SOUTH CHINA SEA

BRUNEI

FIFTH DIVISION

Lawas

Limbang

Seria

Lutong

Miri

Bakenu

Marudi

Niah

Rumah Pasang

Long Seridan

Bakelalan

Pa Lungan
Bario

FOURTH DIVISION

R. Baram

R. Setap

R. Bakong

R. Sibuti

R. Limbang

R. Dapar

Belaga

R. Belaga

R. Balui

R. Linau

R. Kajang

Long Jawai

R. Aput

R. Balui

R. Kliong

Kapit

Nangga Gaat

DIVISION

R. Bangkit

Rajang

KALIMANTAN

Indonesian Borneo)

N

0 10   50   100
                              miles

The Undeclared War

Also by Harold James
& Denis Sheil-Small

THE GURKHAS (Macdonald, 1965)

The Undeclared War

THE STORY OF THE INDONESIAN CONFRONTATION
1962–1966

Harold James
&
Denis Sheil-Small

LEO COOPER · LONDON

First published in Great Britain, 1971 by
LEO COOPER LTD, 196 Shaftesbury Avenue, W.C.2
Copyright © Harold James and Denis Sheil-Small, 1971

ISBN 0 85052 080 0

Printed in Great Britain by
Western Printing Services Ltd, Bristol

CONTENTS

CONTENTS

ILLUSTRATIONS

ACKNOWLEDGEMENTS

This book could not have been written without the most generous help and encouragement from a great number of people. We should first of all like to thank most warmly General Sir Walter Walker, KCB, CBE, DSO for letting us have a great deal of information and for introductions to numerous contacts.

We are also most grateful to Rear-Admiral P. J. Morgan, CB, DSC, RN; Captain B. D. O. MacIntyre, DSO, ADC, RN; Commander G. J. Sherman, MBE, RN and Commander D. F. Burke, MBE, RN for their generous assistance.

Various officers from the Royal Marine Commandos went to great lengths to provide information, and we are most grateful to Major-General F. C. Barton, CB, CBE, RM; Lt-Col P. J. F. Whiteley, OBE, RM; Lt-Col R. J. Ephraums, OBE, RM and Lt D. A. Young, RM.

We are particularly indebted to Brigadier J. B. A. Glennie, CBE, DSO, ADC for invaluable material on the Brunei Revolt, as we are to Colonel W. G. McHardy, MBE, MC, Queen's Own Highlanders, and to Mr Tom Harrisson.

It would not have been possible to write about the fine efforts of the artillery and armoured formations without invaluable assistance from Lt-Col R. Lyon, OBE, RA, and Lt-Col J. A. Cowgill, 4th Royal Tank Regiment.

We are also very much indebted to General J. L. Moulton, CB, DSO, OBE; Lt-Col J. Cross, MBE; Lt-Col D. J. Lear; Col A. G. Haywood, MVO, MC and Mr H. P. Bryson, MC.

Many officers from military formations gave us considerable help and encouragement, and we should like to express our warm thanks to Lt-Col C. W. B. Purdon, MC, Royal Ulster Rifles; Lt-Col J. Neish, The Gordon Highlanders; Lt-Col G. A. C. Cowan, MBE and Major T. R. Holloway from The Royal Anglian Regiment; and Lt-Col C. E. Eberhardie, MBE, MC, The Parachute Regiment.

A great deal of help and encouragement was also received from the Brigade of Gurkhas, and we are much indebted to Lt-Col H. R. K. Gibbs; Lt-Col J. M. C. Thornton, MC; Col C. S. F. Carroll, OBE, MC;

Lt-Col D. F. Neill, OBE, MC; Lt-Col C. G. Wylie; Lt-Col H. G. W. Shakespear, MC; Lt-Col J. C. Davis; Col J. B. Clements, MBE, MC; Brigadier G. B. Proctor; Brigadier P. O. Myers, OBE, MC; Col R. B. E. Upton; Brigadier E. J. S. Burnett, DSO, OBE, MC; Lt-Col A. S. Harvey, OBE, MC; Captain D. K. S. Simons; Major R. N. B. McGurk; Lt-Col J. A. I. Fillingham, OBE; Col R. C. Jackman, OBE; Major C. E. Maunsell, MC; Lt-Col B. F. L. Rooney, OBE; Captain D. T. Henderson-Peal; and Brigadier B. G. Hickey, OBE, MC.

For placing their libraries at our disposal we are most grateful to Mr D. H. Simpson, FLA (Royal Commonwealth Society); Mr D. W. King, OBE, FLA (War Office); Mr J. R. Dineen, ALA (Royal United Service Institution) and to their respective staff.

For their kind and invaluable assistance in searching out photographs we should like to thank Mr D. P. Mayne (Imperial War Museum); Mr G. Goodenough (Royal Navy); Mr J. H. G. Bennett (Royal Air Force) and their respective staff.

Many friends also helped, and we are particularly indebted to Mrs Gillian Watson for typing scores of letters; Mr Leslie Egginton for so kindly assisting with the proof reading; and Mr Hugh Hanning and Mr Tom Pocock for much encouragement.

GLOSSARY

of uncommon abbreviations used in this book

ACPL	Armed Customs Patrol Launch
BCP	Borneo Communist Party
BGS	Brigadier General Staff
BPS	Barisan Pemuda Sarawak
CCO	Clandestine Communist Organization
CONEFO	Conference on New and Emerging Forces
FARELF	Far East Land Forces
FOO	Forward Observation Officer
GPMG	General Purpose Machine Gun
GPO	Gun Post Officer
IBT	Indonesian Border Terrorist
KKO	Korps Komando Operasi (Marine Commandos)
KOGAM	Indonesian for 'Crush Malaysia Command'
KOTI	Indonesian for 'War Council'
LCA	Landing Craft Assault
LCT	Landing Craft Tank
LZ	Landing Zone
PAP	People's Action Party
PGT	Air Force Paratroops (Indonesian)
PKI	Indonesian Communist Party
QGO	Queen's Gurkha Officer
RCL	Ramp Cargo Lighters
RMNS	Royal Malayan Navy Ship
RMR	Royal Malayan Regiment
RNZIR	Royal New Zealand Infantry Regiment
RPKAD	Army Paratroops (Indonesian)
SLR	Self-Loading Rifle
TAG	Tawau Assault Group
TNKU	Tentera Nasional Kalimantan Utara (The North Kalimantan National Army)
TNI	Tentera Nasional Indonesia
WP	White Phosphorus (Grenade)

INTRODUCTION
Background to
an Undeclared War

The birth of Malaysia was a set-back to one man's dangerous dream of a mighty Indonesian empire. This man was Sukarno, President of the Indonesian Republic, and ruler of over 100 million people.

A glance at the map of South-East Asia shows that the territories of Indonesia stretch for over three thousand miles in a vast crescent which encircles the Malay Peninsula, Singapore, Sarawak, and Sabah (North Borneo) on three sides. It was Sukarno's ambition to bring these other territories under his domination.

The dream was born in March 1945 when, with capitulation imminent, the Japanese Military Administrator of Occupied Netherlands East Indies set up a body named the Investigating Committee for the Preparation of Indonesia's Independence. Its fifty-nine members represented all principal and ethnic groups of Java and Madura and included Sukarno and the late Professor Yamin.

At a meeting towards the middle of the year, Professor Yamin electrified the forty-five year old Sukarno with a precise and grandiose definition of Indonesian aspiration. Yamin visualized no less than an Indonesian Empire—an Alliance of countries in the south—consisting of Indonesia, Burma, Thailand, Vietnam, and the Philippines.

'The Malay Peninsula,' he told the meeting, 'forms the neck of our Archipelago. To unite Malaya and Indonesia will strengthen our position and complete our entity and accord.'

The professor's words were fervently endorsed by Sukarno, who said that he saw divine sanction in a pan-Indonesia which would include all the Maphilindo countries (Malaya, Philippines, and Indonesia). Moderates pointed out the dangers of such expansionism, particularly with its racial overtones, and contended that Malaya should be left to decide her own destiny. But Sukarno never forgot that dream, and was determined to make it come true.

In the years which followed, Indonesia won her independence from the Dutch, and Sukarno established himself as virtual dictator. As his power increased he became hypnotized by his vision—and hypnotized most of those about him.

That he was able to rally public opinion to his cause was a reflection of his character. Cast in the mould of a Castro, he had entered politics in 1926 and soon antagonized the Dutch colonial authorities. He served two terms of imprisonment for his political beliefs. The first was of two years' duration. When he was jailed again, in 1933, he was in custody for ten years until released by the Japanese occupation forces. He co-operated with the Japanese until their defeat but, with the return of the Dutch, became involved in open hostilities to achieve an Indonesian Republic. Finally at the Round Table Conference at The Hague in 1949 he was elected President of the new Republic and took up his post in 1950.

Sukarno was a headline addict. An archetypal dictator, he was a flamboyant orator—expressive, humorous in a heavy way, a master of invective and stagecraft. Although many distrusted him, few actively disliked him, on account of his warmth and uninhibited charm. The Indonesian public enjoyed his speeches. If his words became repetitive, if he was conceited, they forgave him, as they forgave him his scandalous private life. His debauchery and extravagance, evidenced by his fantastic private palaces, were bywords. His peccadilloes were what Java had expected of her Sultans, and, in the eyes of the populace, Sukarno was the greatest Sultan of them all. With the good will of his peoples behind him he could have made Indonesia one of the most powerful nations in Asia, but he overreached himself when he tried to bring other countries into his domain.

The man who threatened to thwart Sukarno's ambitions was Tunku Abdul Rahman, descendant of one of Malaya's most aristocratic families. The Tunku was educated at St Catherine's College, Cambridge, and studied law at London's Inner Temple.

Adopting the unusual cause of conservative anti-colonialism he rapidly emerged as a leader of stature, eventually becoming Prime Minister of the Malayan Federation in 1957.

In character and demeanour, the Tunku was the antithesis of Sukarno. Quiet, dignified, almost staid, he dressed inconspicuously in a sarong or in a blue cotton tunic and trousers. But he also had the Malayan characteristics of pride and arrogance. Unlike Sukarno, the master of bluff, once the Tunku adopted a course—as on Malaysia—he was immovable.

A long duel developed between these two leaders. At first there was no open hostility. Sukarno opened the game by trying to turn Malayan public opinion away from Malaysia and towards Indonesia. In November 1958, he sent Brigadier Gusti Djatikusumo to Singapore as the Indonesian Consul-General. The Brigadier, eschewing diplomacy, approached the task of winning support for his country with military bluntness. Under his direction, the Indonesian Consulate, one of the most opulent in the world, became the centre of intelligence activity. Staff were ordered to obtain information about the armed forces in Singapore, and to report to the Consul-General direct. The Indonesian intelligence organization was tightened up in Singapore and on the Peninsula. Agents equipped with miniature cameras, wristwatch microphones, mini tape-recorders, and cine cameras infiltrated RAF establishments as lavatory attendants, room-boys, and waiters. Agents fanned out through Malaya and Borneo, to carry out sabotage and to foment anti-Chinese rioting.

Sukarno's first moves were countered by the Tunku with an announcement which threatened to destroy his dream of empire. On 27 May 1961, in an historic address to the Foreign Correspondents Association of South-East Asia, the Tunku made the first formal reference to *Malaysia* as a desirable, practical possibility.

'Malaya today as a nation realizes that she cannot stand alone. Sooner or later Malaya must have an understanding with Britain and the peoples of the territories of Singapore, North Borneo, Brunei and Sarawak.'

He suggested that a plan be devised 'whereby these territories can be brought closer together in political and economic co-operation'.

Reactions to the Tunku's proposal were swift and favourable in Singapore, Sarawak, and North Borneo; even the British Government saw it as a satisfactory solution of their colonial responsibilities in South-East Asia. It offered speedy independence to Britain's remaining colonies and protectorates in the area and a good chance of security and prosperity in the future.

In Singapore a popular vote gave Prime Minister Lee Kuan Yew the powers to bring the island into the new federation. In Sarawak and North Borneo a commission under Lord Cobbold reported that a large majority of the population in both territories favoured the project, given suitable conditions and safeguards. Even the Indonesian Government appeared to give its support. Foreign Minister Subandrio, speaking in the General Assembly of the United Nations on 20 November 1961, when the Cobbold Commission was appointed, said, 'We are not only disclaiming the territories outside the former Netherlands East Indies, though they are of the same island [Borneo], but—more than that—when Malaya told us of its intention to merge with the three British Crown Colonies of Sarawak, Brunei and North Borneo as one federation, we told them that we had no objections and that we wished them success with this merger so that everyone might live in peace and freedom.'

Moderate his speech may have been but it was mere dust flung in the eyes of world opinion for if Sukarno's dream of *Indonesia Raya* was to come true he must have control of Malaysia. The Foreign Minister was able to make his statement because Sukarno had never openly claimed any part of what was to become Malaysian territory. His basic accusation against Malaya was that she had not shaken off her colonial chains. On the one hand she had filed through the chains to gain independence, yet on the other she seemed reluctant to be completely free of her colonialist 'jailer'—for she kept open trade connections and maintained a defence agreement with Britain. Although this last point antagonized Sukarno the most, he simultaneously criticized Malaya for being too weak to oppose the dangerous southward expansion of Communist China. These contradictory views were typical of the man.

Nevertheless, the Tunku tried to maintain friendly relations with Sukarno. An example of this was provided by the West

Irian affair. West Irian (Dutch New Guinea) was the last stronghold of the Dutch in the East Indies. Sukarno was determined that it should become a part of Indonesia, and a political battle raged for several years. At one stage the Tunku, in an effort to find a compromise, visited The Hague, Washington, and the United Nations. The result of his efforts was a furore in the Indonesian Press, and his visits were attacked in Djakarta as interference. No mention was made of the fact that the Tunku had corresponded in advance with Sukarno and had actually received his encouragement.

When, in 1962, the West Irian problem seemed likely to flare into another war between Indonesia and the Dutch, the Tunku allowed Sukarno to recruit Malay volunteers. Indonesian officials, supported by anti-Malaysian political parties, carried out an extensive recruiting drive which was effective camouflage for active propaganda and for the mobilization of support for Indonesia.

Mass rallies were held in Singapore, and West Irian Relief Committees were set up. Indonesian consular officials from Singapore visited the mainland, whipping up enthusiasm amongst Malays of Indonesian origin. Ultimately, of 300 volunteers registered in Singapore between 5 and 9 April only fifty were selected after a thorough screening. These, together with seventy-three recruits selected from almost 5,000 volunteers from the mainland, were sent to Djakarta for four months' 'military' training, an essential part of which was political indoctrination. Sukarno was built up as leader of the world's 'third strongest military power', in contrast to the Tunku who was accused of being a 'colonial stooge'.

All this training had no relevance to the West Irian problem which was resolved independently in August. Sukarno throughout intended to use these volunteers as recruits for an Indonesian Fifth Column. Most significant was the formation of a clandestine organization among the volunteers which aimed at overthrowing the Malay Government and replacing it with a pro-Indonesian one. Organized in cells of ten and supported by Indonesian arms, they were to create disturbances among the civil population. Members, sworn to secrecy, signed their names in a 'Book of Blood'.

In November 1962, thirty-two volunteers returned to Malaya

and the remainder were abruptly sent back on Christmas Eve. Their sudden dispatch was due to the fear that the Malay Government might suspect the real reason for their training, and forbid their return.

This experiment in recruiting Malays for Indonesian purposes was more of a psychological than a military exercise. Malaya having supported Indonesia in the United Nations over the West Irian issue, Sukarno emerged as an anti-colonial leader whom Malays could follow. It also pioneered a new path of penetration into Malaya.

Sukarno, although always close to the Indonesian Communists, was too much of a nationalist to join the party. In Indonesia he created a socialist régime and was committed to proving it superior to the free-enterprise régime of Malaya. With his bitter resentment at Malaya for clinging to her ties with Britain, his fears of the expansion into South-East Asia of Chinese Communists, and above all his grandiose dream of ruling the entire Archipelago, the rift began to widen.

The Tunku, for all his aristocratic pride, must receive credit for his sustained efforts to bring Indonesia and Malaya closer together; but Sukarno was determined to kill the Malayan tiger and drive off the British lion. His aim was to destroy the Tunku's idea of Malaysia in embryo, or, failing this, to attack it militarily, economically and politically while the infant nation was still learning how to walk.

Towards the end of 1962, Sukarno saw his chance. The Tunku was anxious for Brunei to join Malaysia, but the Sultan of Brunei would not definitely commit himself. Within Brunei there were dissident factions ready to break into open revolt. If the rebellion was successful, it would be bound to cause uncertainties in the bordering countries of Sarawak and North Borneo, and with Indonesian agitators to add to the doubts, the whole conception of Malaysia might be stillborn.

Part One

THE BRUNEI REVOLT

Although the smallest of the Borneo States, Brunei is very wealthy. Economically, the Sultan is almost entirely dependent

ONE
Red Ale

At 1500 on Saturday, 8 December 1962, an RAF Beverley roared down the runway at Seletar on Singapore Island. Rising above the Straits of Johore and the jungle beyond, the aircraft banked east over the Pengarang swamps and headed out over the South China Sea to Borneo. Seven hundred and forty miles away, the Sultanate of Brunei was in the grip of a revolt.

One of the passengers in the aircraft was Major Tony Lloyd-Williams, in command of the 'Initial Force' ordered to the Sultan's aid. Apart from the news that Brunei Police Station had been attacked by a hundred rebels at first light that morning, Lloyd-Williams knew little about the situation. He would be arriving by night in a strange place, perhaps already overrun by rebels. He did not even have a map of the area.

Because the position at Brunei Airfield was uncertain, the aircraft was bound for the RAF Station at Labuan, an island off the Brunei coast. It was hoped that the airfield was still in Government hands, otherwise valuable time would be lost in ferrying the force by sea from Labuan. As the Beverley moved closer to Borneo, Lloyd-Williams wondered what the next few hours would bring.

Brunei thrusts like two fangs into the Fourth and Fifth Divisions of Sarawak. A British Protectorate, ruled by a Sultan, it covers 2,226 square miles and has a population of 85,000. Of these, 45,000 are Malays, 21,000 Chinese, and the remainder are indigenous.

Brunei Town, the captial, is ten miles up the Brunei River—a twisting, tidal stream with numerous sandbanks, and a navigable channel suitable only for minesweepers, LCTs or smaller ships. The eighty-mile coastal belt is fairly well-populated, low-lying, and in places quite open. Inland, thick virgin jungle rises to

3

eight thousand feet within fifty miles of the coast. Along the seaboard is a road which links the more important towns west of the capital. There are a few tracks, leading short distances inland, so the local population depends mainly on the rivers for transport. In the interior a few jungle tracks link the scattered villages, but the terrain is extremely rough, and travel, except by water, is measured in days rather than hours.

Although the smallest of the Borneo States, Brunei is very wealthy. Economically, the Sultan is almost entirely dependent on the Brunei Shell Petroleum Company. The oilfields at Seria, on the coast towards the western border with Sarawak's Fourth Division, produce over four million tons of oil a year.

During 1962 overtures were made to the Sultan, Sir Omar Ali Saifuddin, with a view to Brunei becoming part of Malaysia. In July the Brunei Legislative Council agreed to the proposals, and the Sultan expressed his own support provided the conditions were beneficial to Brunei. His problem was to preserve a feudalistic order while giving it the outward appearance of a parliamentary democracy. Under a new constitution, elections were held for the first time in September, and resulted in an overwhelming victory for the *Partai Ra'ayat* (People's Party). Sixteen representatives were duly sworn in as councillors of the Legislative Assembly; but the other seventeen members were nominated by the Sultan, who thereby retained his supreme authority.

During the elections the Partai Ra'ayat had not opposed Malaysia directly, but had maintained that before any move was made there should be a unification of Brunei, Sarawak and North Borneo, with the Sultan as constitutional ruler. Naturally this proposal appealed to Brunei which had once ruled the whole area; but it ignored the fact that the Malaysian scheme was widely supported by most parties and people in Sarawak and North Borneo. The Partai Ra'ayat also declared its intention to help the Sultan bring about a more liberal constitution. Some of the party leaders, however, formed a secret wing called the *Tentera Nasional Kalimantan Utara* (TNKU)—The North Kalimantan National Army.

The leader of the TNKU was Azahari, thirty-four years of age and of Arab/Malay parentage. At the age of twelve he had been sent by the Japanese to study in occupied Netherlands East

4

Indies. In this atmosphere of rising nationalism his own plans for the future of Brunei took root. Following the defeat of Japan, Azahari fought with the Indonesian anti-Dutch units in Java and Sumatra. In 1952 he returned to Brunei, when he was imprisoned for six months for holding an unlawful meeting.

The 1962 elections gave him the opportunity to take a more legal part in Brunei's affairs, but his sympathy was with Indonesia, and his ambition was to create *Kalimantan Utara* (a new state consisting of Brunei, North Borneo, and Sarawak) with the Sultan as its nominal head.

How much was Azahari influenced by Sukarno? As a young man he had fought alongside Indonesian troops. Since then he had been in touch with Koesto, the head of Indonesian intelligence in Singapore, and in August 1962 he had visited the Indonesian Consul at Jesselton in North Borneo. What actually passed between them at this meeting is not known, but he obviously received encouragement and the promise of moral support, if not actual assistance with arms and ammunition. Sukarno probably did not wish to make his support public, feeling certain that the revolt would succeed and that he could then take a more active role. But the PKI (Indonesian Communist Party) came out in open support as soon as the revolt started, and in view of this the Indonesian Government had to follow suit.

On 20 December, Mr Nigel Fisher, Under-Secretary of State for the Colonies, said in the House of Commons, 'We have noted with concern the expression of sympathy for the rebels made by Indonesian leaders.'

The Indonesian propaganda machinery publicly took up Azahari's cause and treated the Brunei rebellion as an expression throughout North Borneo of popular opposition to joining Malaysia. Within a few weeks of the September elections, the TNKU decided to take control of Brunei. Yassin Affendi was nominated General Officer Commanding the Rebel Forces. Some fifteen companies, each of one hundred and fifty fully-trained soldiers, were organized, and as many again of partly-trained men, giving an active strength of about four thousand. The general standard of training was low, although a number had been trained in Kalimantan and a few had taken special courses in Djakarta. About a thousand were armed with shot-guns, the remainder had only parangs, axes or spears. It was hoped to obtain more modern weapons from the police stations. It was also hoped that success would help to swell the ranks of the revolutionaries. Azahari himself left for Manila before the first shot was fired. Whatever the outcome, he intended to be safe.

At 0930 on 7 December 1962, a reliable informer warned Mr Fisher, Resident of the Fourth Division, that a rebellion was imminent. Fisher at once informed the Sarawak Government, and the warning was passed to Mr Outram and Mr Mathieson, the Commissioners of Police for Brunei and North Borneo respectively. This enabled many immediate precautions to be taken in the three States, and the initial shock of the rebel attacks was countered in some cases with stronger resistance than the rebels had expected.

At 0200 on 8 December, the revolt began in Brunei and East Sarawak. The TNKU plan was to capture the Sultan, all the police stations, and the oilfields. Yassin Affendi, the GOC, and Jais bin Haji Karim, the Military Commander, set up their HQ at Bukit Salileh near Brunei Town. It was their intention to direct the battle by a system of couriers; in fact once the signal for the rebellion was given they had little or no control of events.

In Brunei Town, the rebels captured the power station, cut off the electricity, and attacked the police station with three hundred armed men. Attacks were also launched on the Istana (Sultan's Palace) and on the Prime Minister's House, but thanks to Outram's initiative after the warning these attacks were repulsed. The rebels managed, however, to enter the Residency and capture the acting High Commissioner, Mr W. J. Parks. He was later rescued by Outram himself. The courage and leadership shown by Outram during these first crucial hours seriously hampered the rebel plan. The police recaptured the power station and carried out mopping-up operations, inflicting several casualties and making a number of arrests.

Earlier, Wing Commander Graves, the RAF Commander at Labuan, when warned that trouble was brewing, had sent one of his aircraft to pick up a platoon of the North Borneo Field Force offered by the Government of North Borneo. Their arrival from Jesselton around midday was a welcome addition to Outram's forces.

Although the Commissioner of Police had so far managed to control events in the town, a determined effort by the rebels at this stage could still have proved successful. But they failed to realize the importance of denying the airfield to reinforcements from outside. An attempt was made to block the runway with obstacles, but these were removed by the small group of civilians who held the airfield until the arrival of the North Borneo Field Force contingent.

Westward along the coast the rebels had more success, seizing Tutong and the oilfields at Seria. South of Brunei Town they had control of Limbang and Bangar. But very little of this information was available to the outside world.

Some time before the Brunei Revolt, a contingency plan had been made by HQ 17th Gurkha Division in Seremban. Plan Ale was a standing arrangement to fly into Borneo a small HQ and two rifle companies with internal-security-scale equipment and ammunition, detachments of Royal Engineers and Royal Signals, and a Military Intelligence Officer, to assist civil authorities to restore or maintain law and order. There would be no naval participation unless requested at the alert phase of ordering the plan. The only envisaged build-up of the 'Initial Force' was to send the remainder of the battalion concerned.

When the news of the revolt reached Singapore, Admiral Sir David Luce, Commander-in-Chief of British Forces in the Far East, immediately ordered Plan Ale to be put into execution. The Sultan had called for assistance from Britain under the 1959 Treaty.

The situation did not appear to be urgent or out of hand and at 0400 on the 8th the 99th Gurkha Infantry Brigade was placed on Ale Yellow—forty-eight hours' notice to move. The stand-by battalion was the Queen's Own Highlanders, but the 1/2nd Gurkha Rifles, commanded by Lt-Col Gordon Shakespear, and based at Slim Barracks, Singapore were detailed for the operation. Unfortunately, much of Shakespear's battalion was on detachment at the time. Two platoons were five hundred miles away in North Malaya; the Assault Pioneer Platoon was on concentrated training eighty miles away at Kluang; the Mortar and MMG Sections were on training in South Johore, some thirty miles away but in radio contact. Much of the remainder of the battalion had only recently returned from a wide search on

7

the east coast of Malaya for the navigator of a Javelin fighter which had crashed in that area.

On Saturday the 8th, Shakespear had planned to take on four weeks' jungle training all new riflemen who had been sworn in at the end of their recruit period a month earlier. At 0500, an hour before they were due to leave on the training programme, he was told to stand the battalion to in readiness for movement to Brunei.

Major Lloyd-Williams was ordered to have a small force ready to move by 1600 but long before then the urgency of the situation had become apparent and Red Ale—immediate action —was ordered at 0930. 'Initial Force' was to move as soon as aircraft were available and the rest of the battalion to follow when further aircraft could be provided.

Initial Force HQ and C Company arrived at Seletar Airfield by 1230 and, about the same time, D Company was ready at Changi. But it was Saturday morning and the RAF was not able to provide aircraft immediately. It was not until 1445 hours that the first aircraft took off from Changi with part of D Company— who were supposed to be follow-up troops. Lloyd-Williams took off fifteen minutes later in a Beverley from Seletar, followed by two more Beverley aircraft. The bulk of D Company was lifted from Changi in a Britannia.

When the aircraft entered Labuan control, Major Lloyd-Williams learned that Brunei airfield was not in rebel hands. The three Beverleys changed course for Brunei, but the Britannia and Hastings, carrying D Company, had to land at Labuan, for at this time the runway and airport facilities at Brunei were only large enough for the Beverleys. D Company had to be ferried by smaller aircraft from Labuan as these became available. Brunei Airfield is about two miles north of the town. Arriving in the dark, the troops filtered through in pockets to the Police Station where Lloyd-Williams had established his HQ. By 2300 on the 8th his force consisted of HQ, C Company, and two platoons of D Company.

Some twenty hours after the outbreak of the revolt the bulk of Initial Force had reached Brunei, having flown over a stage length airlift of seven hundred and fifty miles, and subsequent transhipment through Labuan for some of the troops. Considering that neither the Army nor the RAF units were at any stage

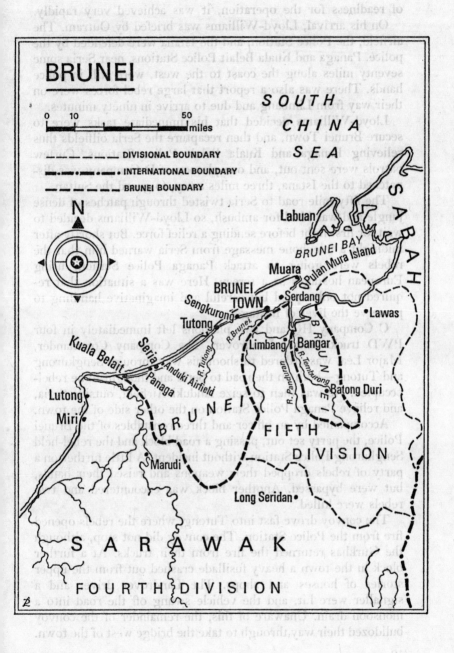

of readiness for the operation, it was achieved very rapidly.

On his arrival, Lloyd-Williams was briefed by Outram. The airfield, the Police Station, and the Istana were defended by the police. Panaga and Kuala Belait Police Stations, near Seria some seventy miles along the coast to the west, were still in police hands. There was also a report that large rebel forces were on their way from Limbang and due to arrive in ninety minutes.

Lloyd-Williams decided that his immediate tasks were to secure Brunei Town, and then recapture the Seria oilfields thus relieving Panaga and Kuala Belait Police Stations. Curfew patrols were sent out, and one platoon of D Company was dispatched to the Istana, three miles away, to guard the Sultan.

The fifty mile road to Seria twisted through patches of dense jungle and was ideal for ambush, so Lloyd-Williams decided to wait for first light before sending a relief force. But shortly after midnight a telephone message from Seria warned him that the rebels were going to attack Panaga Police Station, using European hostages as a screen. Here was a situation that required not only speed but careful and imaginative handling to preserve the lives of hostages.

C Company HQ and two platoons left immediately in four PWD trucks and a Landrover. The Company Commander, Major Lea, was ordered to shoot his way through Sengkurong and Tutong—both on the road to Seria and thought to be rebel-occupied. He was then to seize Anduki Airfield, outside Seria, and relieve Panaga Police Station on the other side of the town.

Accompanied by an officer and three constables of the Brunei Police, the party set out, passing a road block and the rebel-held Sengkurong Police Station without incident. A little further on a party of rebels dropped their weapons and raised their hands, but were bypassed. Another block was encountered and two rebels were killed.

The convoy drove fast into Tutong, where the rebels opened fire from the Police Station. The convoy did not stop, although the Gurkhas returned the fire from their trucks. At a further block in the town a heavy fusillade crashed out from the upper stories of houses and shops. The Landrover driver and a signaller were hit, and the vehicle swung off the road into a monsoon drain. Unaware of this, the remainder of the convoy bulldozed their way through to take the bridge west of the town.

Meanwhile, Lea and his HQ scrambled out of the overturned Landrover to take cover on the veranda of a near-by building. It turned out to be rebel-held and a brief but fierce fight ensued as the Gurkhas engaged their enemy through the ceiling. Obviously this was not the best of positions. Recovering the wireless set from the Landrover, Lea and his men carried the two wounded Gurkhas to a second position in an open fishmarket further down the road—capturing an armed rebel on the way.

During the remainder of the night the two Gurkha platoons, and the rebels, attempted in vain to find C Company HQ. Early next morning the platoons made contact with Lea and proceeded to mop up the town with great thoroughness. Some of the rebels, digging in on high ground above the Police Station, fled when engaged. The rebel casualties totalled seven killed, twenty wounded, and one hundred captured. One Gurkha officer and seven other ranks were wounded.

While Lea was driving to Tutong, Lloyd-Williams was consolidating his position in Brunei Town. At about 0200 on the 9th he received a report that a man was crawling up a monsoon drain near the Government Offices Building. At once a patrol was sent to investigate. Until then everything had been quiet in the town since the Gurkhas had arrived.

Lt David Stephens led the patrol down the dark, unfamiliar approach road. Suddenly firing broke out from the upper stories and rooftops of the Government Offices Building and the Post Office. Stephens fell, mortally wounded. The remainder of the patrol went to ground and returned the fire; simultaneously, the troops and police at the Police Station opened fire across the football ground. Half the platoon remaining in the Police Station then moved quickly to the north-east side of the compound perimeter in anticipation of an attack. But while crossing the open ground they were raked at a range of twenty-five yards by a rebel platoon about to attack the Police Station. A Gurkha officer and four men were wounded, one of whom died later. The remaining Gurkhas reached their positions safely and the rebel assault was repulsed.

Meantime, part of D Company under Major Watterton was approaching the town from the airfield. It had reached the eastern end of the Government Offices when the firing broke

11

out. Watterton, having no idea of the layout of the town, thought the Government Offices Building was the Police Station, and halted his men in order not to come under fire from his own troops. A wireless message from the Police Station orientated him and he was instructed to attack the Government Offices from the rear. Watterton sent one of his platoons forward to attack, but at that moment they were fired at from behind and had to turn to deal with the new threat. In the middle of the firing, uniformed men were seen some two hundred yards north, crossing the road along which the company had just come. Not being aware of the position of the Gurkha patrol which had left the Police Station earlier, it was decided not to open fire. As it turned out, they were, in fact, rebels. It was obvious now that the danger of D and C Companies clashing in the dark was too great, and Watterton was told to lie up till daylight.

At first light (0630) on the 9th, Watterton cleared the buildings east towards the river, and then south towards the Brunei Hotel, taking fourteen prisoners—who later turned out to be police! The remaining platoon of D Company arrived at dawn and searched the Government Offices, capturing four rebels. By nine o'clock the Gurkhas and police were in control, with the important buildings cleared, and sentries posted on rooftops and top floors.

A good deal of blood was found on the veranda of the Government Offices, and from information received later it was assessed that at least twenty-four rebels had been killed during the night of the 8th. In Brunei Town the Gurkhas had lost two killed and four wounded. In the circumstances their casualties could be considered light. They had been given the unenviable task of clearing a completely strange town at night, and against an enemy about whose potential they knew next to nothing.

On the morning of 9 December, Lt-Col Shakespear arrived in Brunei Town to take over from Lloyd-Williams. He brought A Company with him, but this was immediately ferried by Borneo Airways and Shell aircraft to secure the airfield and oilfield at Lutong, and the oilfield at Miri. Shakespear was left with his HQ and C and D Companies (B Company was still in transit and did not arrive until the 10th).

At this stage, Shakespear, like everyone else, thought that he was facing a good guerrilla enemy up to the standards of the communist terrorists in the Malayan emergency. There was still a complete lack of reliable information.

'Everything was rumour,' said Shakespear. 'The Commissioner of Police was very helpful, but since communications were not very good they and we ourselves were all guessing as to what was going on. Rumours in the East are a very strong weapon used by unscrupulous people. It was impossible—certainly on that first day—for me to find out whether these rumours were in fact rumours or had some truth in them.'

Because of this lack of definite information, Shakespear decided to postpone the Seria operation and recalled C Company from Tutong. He knew that Brunei Town was secure and that he could retain control of it and of the airfield. His intention was to work outwards and gather his own information. He also decided to evacuate the women and children as he had no men to spare for guard duties over a wide area.

'These may have seemed slightly retrograde steps,' he said later, 'but there were numerous reports of a thousand insurgents forming up to attack this place or that, and Brunei Town was the seat of Government. The Sultan was the Head and had to be guarded. Besides the shortage of troops, all we had to move in—apart from one or two Landrovers and command vehicles—were PWD tippers. We had not as yet commandeered boats—we hadn't the time—nor were helicopters available for deployment as HMS *Albion* had not arrived at this stage. All the roads and rivers which I had seen were ideal for ambush and this was what we expected from a tough, hard enemy. We were, therefore, dancing to the insurgents' tune for some days. I wanted to regain the initiative as soon as I could.'

Shakespear's HQ was established in the Police Station, but this quickly proved unsuitable for there was no place within the HQ where he could get away and think quietly.

'We all moved rather naturally to the Police Station during the first night as we had to liaise. This is a cardinal error when moving in to quell a rebellion, and as soon as possible one should go to other places and so divert attention from one spot. In fact at first light on the 9th this is what happened and we went out into the town. If only we had had a town plan to look at the mistake would have been avoided.

13

'In the Police Station I saw for the first time a huge town plan of Brunei, but because it was on its side it disorientated me completely for quite a long time and I thought that east was north and north was west, which was disturbing to say the least. The scale was in yards to a chain which was unfamiliar and I got the impression that Brunei Town was larger than in fact it was.'

During the 9th, the town and airfield were consolidated by energetic patrolling and the tactical disposition of troops on rooftops, at road junctions, and at bridges to prevent rebel infiltration. The security of the Sultan was all-important but it needed many troops to guard the Istana, so he was persuaded to move into the Police Station where he stayed with his immediate entourage for the next twenty-four hours. An effective twenty-four hour curfew was imposed, and several attempts by rebels to infiltrate the town during the night of the 9th/10th were severely dealt with.

In Singapore on Sunday, 9 December, Admiral Luce gave Brigadier Glennie (BGS HQ/FARELF) his instructions: 'You will proceed to Brunei and take command of all land, sea and air forces in the Borneo Territory and you will restore the situation.'

As Glennie remarked later, 'Surely the clearest order any soldier ever received since Caesar invaded Gaul.'

The brigadier scrambled an *ad hoc* staff. 'My Staff HQ was like the teams at the best Inter-Services game at Twickenham, but with all three Services on the same side.' At 1100 on Sunday he left Singapore with his HQ, arriving in Labuan by 1930 the same day. He was quickly followed by the Air Task Force Commander, Group Capt R. D. Williams.

Glennie decided to stay the night at Labuan because of the curfew in Brunei Town and the risk of ambush on the road from Brunei airfield to the Police Station. The following morning he established his HQ at the Police Station, which by now was so overcrowded that Shakespear thankfully moved to the Civic Centre.

With Brunei Town secure, Glennie had to decide on the next step. Obviously the Security Forces would have to move outward to regain control of the whole area. With the limited number of troops under command at this stage he had to choose the most important target. Seria, with its vital oilfields, was the obvious choice. The task was finally allotted to the 1st Battalion The Queen's Own Highlanders.

TWO

Action at Seria

At 0315 on 8 December, the rebels captured Seria Police Station and gained control of the oilfields. The European inhabitants were confined to their houses, but later about forty-five hostages, including some Eurasians and Asians were taken to the Police Station. Others were isolated at their places of work in the oilfields.

At 0400 the rebels attacked Panaga Police Station but were repulsed. Later that evening they tried again, this time using their hostages as a human shield. The police opened fire, and one Eurasian was killed and five other hostages wounded.

Further west was the town of Kuala Belait, and here too the police repulsed an attack at 1930 on the 8th. Earlier that day, the rebels occupied the all-important Anduki airfield, situated about a mile east of Seria, and drove some vehicles on to the runway to put it out of action.

That same morning in Singapore, Lt-Col W. G. McHardy, commanding the 1st Bn The Queen's Own Highlanders, had been warned to have two companies ready to move to Brunei. It was thought that an initial force would not move before 0600 on the 10th. But the departure date was advanced to the 9th. Shortly after 1400, one platoon was on its way from Seletar in a Beverley, McHardy and the rest of the company taking off from Changi in a Hastings and arriving in Labuan at 0230 on the 10th.

McHardy was briefed by Glennie before being ferried to Brunei Airfield where the advance platoon had already arrived. A second company sailed from Singapore aboard HMS *Cavalier* at 2000 on the 9th.

The following morning Glennie arrived at Brunei, and confirmed McHardy's task. He emphasized that speed was essential in order to compensate for the small numbers of men on the ground. Some forty minutes later McHardy—together with

Major I. D. Cameron, Outram, and two representatives from the Brunei Shell Petroleum Company—left in a Twin Pioneer to reconnoitre Seria and Kuala Belait. Soon after take-off they received a message that Panaga and Kuala Belait Police Stations were still holding out, although hard pressed.

Following this reconnaissance, McHardy decided to launch two simultaneous attacks. One, west of Seria, was intended to relieve Panaga Police Station, the other to recapture Anduki airfield. Five Twin Pioneer aircraft and a Beverley were available to fly the troops into these locations. An Army Air Corps Beaver was also detailed which McHardy decided to use to co-ordinate the activities of both forces, which would land ten miles apart.

The exit door of each aircraft was removed, and the Highlanders practised rapid de-planing and deployment drill. Shortly after midday on the 10th, the troops boarded their aircraft for the real operation. They carried skeleton battle order only to ensure fast movement immediately after de-planing in Anduki. The ninety men in the Beverley were carried standing in the belly of the aircraft.

Flt-Lt Fenn handled his Beverley brilliantly, bringing the heavy aircraft in low over the sea. The beach came in sight fast, a blur of yellow beneath the wheels. Then, full throttle for the plane to make a sharp rise over the coconut trees fringing the sand to touch down within a few feet of the start of the runway. Quickly he reversed the thrust of the propellers, braking hard at the same time, and the aircraft screamed to a halt less than a quarter of the way down the runway.

The assault party under Capt Macdonald de-planed at high speed, and as the last man jumped out Fenn took off. Although quickly airborne, he was fired at from the area of the airfield buildings. The plane was hit, but not seriously, and he flew safely back to Brunei.

Macdonald straightway moved his force up the airfield, and about two hundred and fifty yards short of the buildings the leading sections came under rifle fire. A few rebels were flushed from around the Control Tower area before the force could advance to clear Anduki Police Post at the entrance to the airfield, killing two rebels and capturing five.

Having cleared the airfield, Macdonald set off up the road to

Seria to complete the second part of his task—the capture of the Bailey Bridge over the Sungei Bera, about one and a half miles west of the airfield. On the way, two rebel vehicles drove up from the town, obviously bringing up reinforcements. The nine occupants of the vehicles were taken prisoner, together with an assorted collection of rifles, shotguns, parangs and tear gas bombs.

A short while later a Landrover was seen approaching fast down the road towards the airfield. The Highlanders rushed to cover in the hope of laying an ambush, but the rebel driver turned the vehicle round and accelerated back up the road. Sergeant Lewis jumped out of the ditch and fired, the rifle bullets hitting the right-hand rear tyre which blew up. The vehicle slewed to a standstill and three armed rebels jumped out. Another snapshot from Lewis and one fell wounded in the groin. The others scattered left and right into the jungle, but not before one was wounded. Both wounded rebels were taken prisoner.

The platoon then moved up to the Bailey Bridge and took up positions on either bank of the river. Meanwhile, a rebel in a civilian car had been shot dead when he tried to rush towards Seria past a post established by Battalion HQ at the entrance to the airport. By 1530 Macdonald's force was established at the Bailey Bridge and had also secured the Shell Explosives Area near by.

Ten miles away the other prong of the attack had by now gone into action. The five Twin Pioneer aircraft of 209 Squadron were personally accompanied by Wing Cdr Graves in the leading aircraft. This group consisted of sixty men under command of Major Cameron.

The landing zone was rough, grassy, and very soft. The sky was darkening quickly with the approach of a tropical storm as the leading pilot came in over some high trees from the north and finally pulled up ten yards short of a ditch and facing a 'Major Road Ahead' sign. Graves at once ordered the other aircraft to land from the south. Even this route was difficult, as it involved brushing the top foliage of a badly-placed tree with the port wing, but thanks to the skill and tenacity of the pilots the first three aircraft landed within fifteen minutes. The last two aircraft were caught by the heavy rainstorm, but eventually made the touchdown. By this time the grass was a mess of churned-up mud, and the last aircraft became temporarily bogged down, but managed to take off again. The whole landing operation had taken twenty-five minutes.

As soon as each group had de-planed, it moved east for about two miles along the road towards Panaga Police Station, which the leading troops entered by 1500 without rebel opposition. Complete surprise had been achieved and the police were delighted to greet their liberators.

Half an hour later, one platoon established a road block about three-quarters of a mile further east along the Jalan Tengah—a main road running through the town to Anduki airfield on the other side. The other platoon was ordered to establish a road block in the area of the Telecommunications Centre on the Jalan Utara—parallel to and north of the Jalan Tengah. 2nd Lt MacKenzie moved his platoon by bounds with two sections abreast. The leading sections reached the penultimate bound without incident, and were within sight of the Telecommunications Centre when they were fired at from a window to the right of the entrance.

Cpl Shepherd brought his Bren gun into action, while L/Cpl Walkinshaw's section doubled forward to engage the rebels from a ditch in front of the building. The heaviest fire was coming from windows on either side of the door. There was a wire enclosure around the building, and MacKenzie decided to get in from the rear. Joined by L/Cpl Ward, he started to climb the wire. Immediately two rebels in the rear building came out with their hands up. One was ordered to double round and open the gate, which he did. Shooting broke out again from the building. Ordering covering fire, MacKenzie doubled forward to a window. With the recklessness of youth, he rashly attempted to locate the rebels by looking through the window. A shot fired from the back of the room grazed his ear.

Following this single shot, however, two rifles were thrown out of the window and two rebels marched out, hands held high. There was still movement inside, but the surrendered rebels called out to their compatriots and the remainder came out. Altogether eight rebels were captured and four hostages released. The building was searched, and a road block dug and occupied.

Within an hour a car approaching from the west was stopped,

and three rebels were arrested. Ten minutes later a green Hillman van, flying Partai Ra'ayat flags, approached from the east, flashing its lights three times. A burst from Cpl Mac-Donald's Bren and the driver stopped the van, backed and tried to turn. Another burst and the van dropped backwards into a ditch. A man ran out and was severely wounded. He and two more rebels were taken prisoner.

At 1700 a black Ford saloon drove towards the road block, flashed its lights three times but spotted the Bren gun. A rifle shot whined overhead. The Bren immediately replied, wounding the two passengers.

During the next half-an-hour, four more rebels were captured, two on a Vespa scooter and two in a Landrover. There followed a long break until shortly after 2300 when a Landrover crashed into the ditch following a burst from the Bren. Two more rebels were taken prisoner. This brought the road block's bag to fifteen rebels, several rifles, shot-guns, and other military equipment, together with enough vehicles to set up as second-hand car dealers.

Before nightfall two more aircraft landed at Anduki, bringing three Landrovers and trailers, the Assault Pioneer Platoon and the Rev J. Stuart. The Padre brought with him a consignment of flares for lighting the flare-path to guide in further Twin Pioneers due to land during the night, truly a case of 'Lighten our Darkness, we beseech Thee, O Lord'!

The weather was still appalling, with rain lashing across the runway, but the pilots kept on flying, and three more aircraft arrived during the early part of the night. At dawn B Company flew in from Labuan where they had arrived after a fast and very rough sea crossing. The scene was now set for the next phase of the operation.

Shortly after their arrival at Anduki, B Company, commanded by Major Wimberley, moved into action, swinging north and then west again on to the coast road—the Jalan Utara. There were oil installations to the south and a narrow strip of rough ground and sea to the north. At first the area was deserted, but then some cars were seen shadowing the column from the main road. Following a show of force, one car surrendered at a distance of sixty yards without a fight. Near an oil installation, a section was fired at by a band of rebels, but on being engaged the rebels fled, some on foot, some by car. One man was hit, but escaped. Most of these rebels were armed only with parangs, but a few carried firearms. Another party of natives waved a white flag frantically and were found to be oil employees who had been ordered to carry on working since they controlled the local electricity supply; they were allowed to continue their work.

By midday a strongpoint was established at the crossroads near the Shell Materials Area which was sited between the Jalan Utara and the sea. Some European and Asian Shell employees, who had been held in their offices since the 8th, hung out a Union Jack. They were able to give information on local rebel strongpoints.

The Materials Area was manned by Company HQ, the MMG Platoon, and the Mortar Section. The remainder of the company advanced westwards for a mile or so to establish a further strongpoint at the Community Centre.

Meanwhile, 6 Platoon continued towards the Roxana Cinema with 5 Platoon in reserve. A Landrover suddenly appeared and the driver was shot through the head. The vehicle plunged into a ditch, its two-way radio still working. More rebels were rounded up following accurate information supplied by a local Malay. At 1400 contact was made with 3 Platoon of A Company who had moved east during the morning from the road block near the Telecommunications Centre. A clear route from Anduki to the western end of Seria was thus established.

Earlier that day, McHardy had ordered Cameron to establish a firm road block in the area of the Brunei Police Barracks some three-quarters of a mile west of the Twin Pioneer Landing Zone. As the police were reluctant to operate alone, Cameron decided to move 2 Platoon from the road block near Panaga Police Station, and to command the mixed force personally. The Highland platoon and two sections of Brunei Police set out in vehicles, but soon a Landrover appeared in the far distance, turned, and disappeared. Taking no chances, Cameron ordered his men to de-bus. 2 Platoon took the lead, moving in broken arrowhead formation on either side of the road. After the first half-mile, Cameron realized that the police were not following, and they were quickly brought to heel. Moving fast, 2 Platoon reached the roundabout just beyond the Landing Zone. The leading section doubled across the roundabout and started off down the Kuala Belait road towards the Police Barracks. About a quarter of a mile beyond the roundabout was the luxurious Istana Kota Menggalela—the Sultan's country palace.

A car suddenly drove out of the palace grounds. The leading section opened fire at a hundred yards range, hitting the car several times. It rolled into the ditch, and the driver, obviously seriously wounded, fell out of the door. But before he could be taken prisoner, a rebel strongpoint in the Istana opened fire with a Bren gun and several rifles. The Highlanders took cover and returned the fire. The wounded driver escaped during the ensuing battle. Cameron ordered the two rear sections to fan out on the right flank and the police were given the task of watching the beach at the north of the palace.

The two Highland sections leapfrogged towards the Istana through a strip of jungle until they reached a driveway. Remaining at the forward edge of the jungle, one section opened fire. Under cover of this, Cameron, with Lt McCall and two men all armed with tear gas grenades, ran to the edge of the building. Cameron and McCall threw their grenades through a ground floor window. Then McCall, moving round a corner, came almost face to face with an armed rebel and shot him in the centre of the body. After this brief action the party returned quickly to the jungle strip. It was hoped that the tear gas would persuade the rebels to surrender, but five minutes later they intensified their fire and it was obvious that they were going to fight it out.

One section now moved up parallel to the sea along a line of trees and near enough for some of the men to run up to the bay windows and throw in tear gas grenades. But these rebels were the most determined that had been met so far. They were apparently well-equipped and had a good supply of ammunition; Bren and rifle bullets continued to stream out of the Istana.

Cameron now decided that he would have to force an entry into the building. Accompanied by McCall and one section, he approached the house again from the jungle strip. Without opposition they reached a balcony outside the bay windows covering all the windows on that side of the building. Leaving the section to cover them from the balcony, Cameron and

McCall climbed in through a window and entered a large room which was empty. They cleared two other rooms on the ground floor, finding in one of them a wounded rebel—shot earlier by McCall—who surrendered. The section now entered the house and followed Cameron as he moved up the gilt staircase. A rebel appeared on the landing with his hands raised. Opening the door of a room on the first floor Cameron found himself confronted by five armed rebels. He fired a shot over their heads and the men promptly raised their hands in surrender! The rest of the house was cleared room by room. A dead sniper was found on the roof, and a rebel was captured in some buildings to the rear of the Istana, bringing the total of rebel losses to one killed and eight captured. During the attack five more had rushed out of the building. Two were wounded but escaped. The other three were seen by the police who did not fire. Eight rifles, one Bren, a Sten, tear gas grenades, and a large supply of ammunition and police uniforms were recovered.

From the Istana, 2 Platoon continued its advance towards the Police Barracks. Before entering the buildings, it was decided to repair two Brens which had jammed during the Istana battle. A sergeant had just finishing repairing the second when a car approached. He tested the gun with one shot through the windscreen which grazed the side of the passenger's head. The driver, armed with a shot-gun, bravely, but in the circumstances rather foolishly, leapt out and ran towards the platoon. He had taken only a few steps when he was shot dead.

The platoon cleared the barracks, which had been ransacked, and completed their task by pulling down the rebel flag. Then they moved back down the road and took up defensive positions covering all three roads leading to the roundabout.

McHardy was reinforced by a company of the 1/2nd Gurkhas under Major Bowring with orders to clear Kuala Belait. Bowring moved his force towards the outskirts of the town where his men de-bussed to avoid the danger of ambush. Advancing on foot, the Gurkhas systematically cleared the outskirts under intermittent sniping. One rebel was taken prisoner.

The rebel strongpoint was the Government Offices Building which dominated the town. Just before darkness the Gurkhas cleared the building of rebels and took up positions in the area for the night. McHardy sent forward a platoon of the

Highlanders to reinforce Bowring's command and both Gurkhas and Highlanders passed a comparatively quiet night.

The following morning the Gurkha company broke the back of rebel resistance in Kuala Belait and rescued four European hostages from the Police Station. Members of the police who had dispersed during the previous days were contacted, and although very nervous and frightened of reprisals to their families, were quickly reassured by the presence of the Gurkhas.

Gradually, McHardy had closed the cordon around the Seria Police Station and bazaar in the centre of the town where the rebels had their main stronghold. In order to maintain better observation of the rebels in that quarter, the Highlanders established a radio station and observation point on top of an oil derrick. In the vital Shell installations, many local employees who had remained at their posts manning essential services were desperately short of food. The Highlanders supplied them with rice and boxes of *compo* rations, and also escorted Shell employees into installations to switch on certain main valves, the filtration plant, and deep-freezing equipment. Snipers from the rooftops of Seria bazaar fired on some of these parties at ranges from one to two hundred yards but no one was hit.

At last light on Tuesday, 11 December, the layout of McHardy's force was as follows:

East of Seria, the situation as before at the Anduki airfield, the Bailey Bridge, and the Explosives Area. To the north, the Shell Transport Area and the Community Centre were still held. In the west, there were strongpoints at the Panaga Police Station, the roundabout near the Istana Kota Menggalela, and the Roxana Cinema.

The Highlanders were now ready to complete their most difficult task, clearing the bazaar and Seria Police Station without causing harm to the many hostages still in captivity.

According to intelligence reports there were about two hundred armed rebels in the bazaar and Police Station, of whom some fifty were 'hard-core'. The hostages were believed to be in the Police Station, guarded by rebels at the gates of the compound and in positions under the timber bungalows to the south of the compound. It was also known that the rebels had established strongpoints on the roofs of several tall shops and houses in the centre of the bazaar.

During the morning of the 12th, many eye-witness accounts of rebel movements in and around the Police Station were telephoned to Battalion HQ. The detailed reports were gathered by Mr B. Levick of Shell, who passed on a mass of useful information to McHardy. A serious problem which faced the Highlanders' colonel was a report that the fifty 'hard-core' rebels might well murder the hostages if cornered. Because of this, he deliberately avoided completely surrounding the last rebel stronghold in Seria. Instead he ordered Macdonald to move his force from the Explosives Area through the jungle to establish hidden cut-off positions astride the railway running south-east from the town, and to cover an east–west ride cut through the jungle about a mile south. These ambushes had to be established by 1100.

At 1115 6 Platoon, together with the MMG Platoon and the Mortar Section, moved on foot from the Community Centre. With 6 Platoon in the lead they advanced south for one block, then swung left to approach the Police Station from the west. Observation was difficult because of the large number of abandoned cars and lorries, but figures were seen scurrying to and fro across the road. Two hundred yards from their objective, the force reached the Malay School and a block of flats without opposition. 6 Platoon held the area, while the Mortar Section mounted Bren guns on the rooftops of both these buildings. Accompanying the force was Inspector Mustapha of the Brunei Police, with instructions to call on the rebels to surrender. This he proceeded to do through a powerful loud-hailer, advising them that resistance was useless, and that anyone who laid down his arms and came out into the open would not be shot. His plea was unsuccessful.

The MMG Platoon then advanced by sections towards the Police Station, Lt Taylor moving with the leading group to control the fire if necessary. He had instructions to get into the Police Station as quickly as possible with the greatest show of force, but with the minimum of firing. Fifty yards from their objective they were met by rifle shots and bursts of automatic fire from a Sterling in a prepared position under a house. The fire was returned and at least two men were seen to duck between the timber buildings. As the men crossed the road they were shot at again by the Mortar Section on the rooftops.

At this moment four RAF Hunters started to 'beat up' the area according to plan. While the jets screamed overhead, the MMG Platoon continued to advance cautiously until one section covered the front of the Police Station from a monsoon drain at a range of twenty yards, and another section and Platoon HQ covered the crossroads outside. Movement was seen through the doors and windows of the Police Station.

Taylor, with the reserve section of the MMG Platoon, then climbed over a seven-foot wire fence some distance to the rear, and led a rush into the building. The arms *kote* (store) and one of the cells were found to be full of hostages sitting on the floor. In another room were five rebels—two wounded, who surrendered—a Shell doctor, and a nurse. There were thirty hostages in the kote and sixteen in the one-man cell. All very crowded, but all safe. The gates at the front were then forced open, and while the MMG Platoon held the building, 6 Platoon cleared the Police Barracks, finding no rebels, but plenty of rifles, shot-guns, and ammunition.

Before the area could be declared safe, or the surrounding buildings properly searched, the press arrived in a fleet of Landrovers. Chaos ensued with reporters, hostages, and house-clearing Highlanders all mixed up together. Luckily the rebels had withdrawn, but B Company spent a further three hours clearing all the houses surrounding the Police Station. Although nearly all the rebels had escaped through the gap to the south, this probably saved the hostages from harm. In any event, most of the rebels were captured within the next few days.

McHardy, ably supported by his officers and men, had carried out a difficult assignment with complete success. It was a brilliant plan, well executed. The Queen's Own Highlanders suffered not a single casualty, and no hostage was harmed from the time the battalion entered the area on the evening of the 10th.

THREE

'They'll be Wearing Dark Green Bonnets . . .'

The operations in Brunei were a fine example of teamwork by all three Services. On 11 December, two Coastal Minesweepers, HMS *Fiskerton* and HMS *Chawton*, arrived from Singapore and were immediately formed as one unit, sharing various duties between them. *Fiskerton*'s Commanding Officer appointed himself Harbour Master, Brunei. This entailed control and operations of all boat traffic, including those used in operations at Limbang, Bangar, Muara, and the Lawas area. *Chawton*'s Commanding Officer became the Naval Supply Officer. He and his crew searched high and wide to commandeer everything which floated, including a petrol bowser, longboats, and outboard engines with the necessary fuel. White ensigns were hoisted on all these craft. 'They must have had an amazing number of white ensigns aboard the minesweepers,' Glennie remarked later.

The running of the local harbour craft was expected to be handled by the Port Operating Squadron, RE, but due to air-lift priorities they did not arrive for about a week. It fell to the officers and crews of these two small ships to man all craft. During major operations personnel on shipboard were reduced at times to half-a-dozen. The energy and initiative shown by the ships' companies in their many extraneous duties contributed in good measure to the success of the operations.

Fiskerton also played her part when the communications network to Singapore failed at the start of the operations. Virtually continual contact was maintained with Singapore either by passing traffic direct or using HMS *Woodbridge Haven* or HMS *Albion* as a link ship. *Fiskerton*'s captain lived with his telephone which was carried around the ship wherever he went, and this meant that for some two weeks he was unable to go ashore except for operational meetings.

The Royal Navy also patrolled the waterway between the Brunei coast and Labuan to stop rebels from escaping by sea. Lt-Cdr Tate, the Naval Liaison Officer, took over the island of Pulan Mura at the entrance to the bay, and used local craft manned by armed sailors to control all shipping. At night an Army Air Corps Auster patrolled the area; if the pilot spotted the wake of any boats he would drop flares.

The presence of the 23,000 ton Commando Ship HMS *Albion*, commanded by Capt Madden, was a considerable asset. The ship's helicopter squadrons were invaluable in positioning and maintaining stops in the jungle, and the maintenance of all mobile forces operating away from their unit bases. Prisoners, police, tracker dogs, interrogation teams, casualties and captured weapons were all air-lifted as required.

The logistic support from *Albion* included fresh bread (2,000 lb a day), the *Albion Advertiser* (2,000 copies daily), tool kits for impressed craft, and rice for Iban tribes inland. The fact that her helicopter squadrons were supporting such a large number and variety of units tested her operations staff considerably, but all demands for support were invariably met quickly and efficiently.

In the first few days of the operation, small RAF staffs worked to the point of exhaustion to keep aircraft flying. In the thirteen-day period occupied by the major phase of operations, the RAF air-lifted the main force from Singapore in 167 sorties during which time the aircraft carried 3,209 passengers, 113 vehicles, 78 trailers, 13 dogs, 2 Auster aircraft, 1 Refueller (31,000 lb) and 624,308 lb of equipment or freight. Within Borneo, transport aircraft made 546 sorties, carrying 4,751 passengers and casevacs (casualty evacuations), and 1,189,160 lb of freight in a total flying time of 707 hours 5 minutes. On offensive operations, Hunters carried out 52 sorties; civilian aircraft also played their part, making 69 sorties. So, in the thirteen-day period, 837 sorties were flown by the RAF and civilian aircraft, carrying 8,000 passengers and casevacs, and 1,800,000 lb of freight. But the aircraft were over-flown to meet the operational requirements, and could not have been maintained much

1. Borneo is a country of dense jungle, countless rivers, swamps, and massive tree-clad hills.

2. The longhouse is synonymous with Borneo, and is a village within a village. This Iban longhouse lodges one hundred families.

3. Confrontation brought the modern world into the Borneans' backyard. These Kelabits soon grew accustomed to having a helicopter pad near their village, and some of the young tribesmen added a helicopter design to the customary tattooing on their bodies.

4. Winning the confidence and trust of the people played an important part in the plan for victory. Here, Iban girls show their Gurkha visitors the local dances.

longer. It was fortunate that activity in Brunei began to tail off when it did.

The standard of flying and flying discipline, despite limited facilities, was extremely high; the courage and endurance displayed of the highest order. Similarly, technical personnel worked intensively with little rest and sleep for long hours. Despite the conditions, serviceability was maintained at the extremely high level of ninety per cent throughout the period. These high rates of effort were made possible by the rapid and effective support from Far East Air Force resources and personnel.

In the opening stages of the operations Brigadier Glennie was able to exercise command with the *ad hoc* arrangements, but he was obviously not staffed or equipped to organize the protracted operations over a greater area with the much larger force which later arrived. It soon became obvious that he would have to delegate some of his responsibilities. In Brigadier Patterson, the dynamic commander of 99 Gurkha Infantry Brigade, the right man was available, and he was appointed to take over command of Land Forces Brunei and East Sarawak on 11 December.

At this time Brunei Town was under control, and the Highlanders were reaching the successful climax of their operation against Seria. Patterson now had to decide on the next important move with the troops available, and with others still arriving piecemeal. South of Brunei Town, the situation in Limbang was vague. To the west, beyond Seria and over the border into the Fourth Division, Lutong and Miri needed consolidating. The most immediate and urgent operation, however, was obviously the recapture of Limbang. This task was given to 42 Commando, Royal Marines.

Limbang, headquarters of the Fifth Division, was situated on the Sungei Limbang, twelve miles south of Brunei Town. The Resident was Mr R. D. Morris, and there was a small European community. The town was some seven-hundred yards long and one-hundred yards wide, carved out of the jungle which surrounds it on three sides, while the fourth borders on the river. Communications were limited to the river and to a few tracks through the jungle. Although small and isolated, the town represented British authority in that part of Sarawak. Accordingly, the TNKU made it one of their targets.

The man chosen to lead the two-hundred-plus insurgents against Limbang was a tough, bearded young rebel named Salleh bin Sambas, who had once served as a policeman in the Sarawak Police Force. By 0200 on 8 December, he had positioned his men at all the key points which included the Police Station, the Gaol, and the Resident's House. Then at a given signal the attack was launched. The police fought bravely until almost daylight, but four were killed and several wounded, and in the end they were overrun. Limbang Gaol was also captured and two important TNKU members, Salleh Kerrudin and Haji Pilok, were released. Until his arrest, Salleh Kerrudin had been designated to lead the rebels against the town. Now he assumed command and appointed Haji Pilok as his second-in-command. Salleh bin Sambas was placed in charge of the Police Station.

The Europeans, including Morris and his wife, were quickly rounded up and thrown in Limbang Gaol where they were detained until the late afternoon of the 11th. The Resident, his wife, and six hostages were then transferred to Limbang Hospital which had been turned into a detention centre. The Hospital and the Police Station formed the centre and pivot of the rebels' defences, and were manned by about one company. The other two companies were deployed along the river bank and in the jungle fringes. The rebels were expecting an attack; their overall military commander, Yassin Affendi, had passed through the town on his way to Temburong District having realized that the cause was lost.

The rebels at Limbang, however, consisted of the toughest and most ruthless core of the TNKU, and they were determined to make a stand. They also believed that because of their large numbers and the added advantage the hostages afforded, they would be able to resist any attack. At the same time, their leaders obviously did not intend staying too long, and there had already been talk of executing the hostages. Morris was well aware that the lives of the hostages were poised on a knife's edge. He felt certain that assistance from outside would arrive either on the evening of the 11th or the morning of the 12th and in a room at the Hospital—turned into Cell No. 1—Morris and his wife considered the problem of how best to avoid being shot by would-be rescuers. They decided that help would come either from the Royal Marines or from the Paratroops so the Morrises composed a verse:

'They'll be wearing dark green bonnets when they come, when they come,
They'll be wearing dark green bonnets when they come,
They'll be wearing dark green bonnets but they won't be singing sonnets.
They'll be wearing dark green bonnets when they come.'

Just in case, they also prepared suitable words for the Red Berets.

At two minutes past six on the morning of the 12th, Morris heard the sound of powerful marine engines, and also of shouted commands from the direction of the Police Station. By standing on his bed, he could just see over the translucent glass in the windows. In the pale light of approaching dawn he made out the form of two Ramp Cargo Lighters. Hurriedly he and his wife put into operation the plan they had worked out. They moved their beds to a location defiladed from any fire which might come through the door, and crawled under them. They had only just reached cover when a machine gun opened fire from the Police Station and was answered from the direction of the river. The window shattered as a fusillade of shots crashed through the glass—not all of it from the attacking troops, for the rebels let loose a couple of charges of buckshot.

With mouths dry from the brick and plaster dust which filled the room, Morris and his wife began to sing.

At 0630 on the 11th, Lt-Col E. R. Bridges, commanding 42 Commando Royal Marines, arrived at Brunei airfield with his Tactical HQ and elements of L Company. He was met by Brigadier Patterson and warned that his Commando would be required to relieve Limbang and Bangar. Bridges at once ordered Lt Davis of L Company to find suitable craft for the operation. During the forenoon the colonel, with his Intelligence Officer, made an air reconnaissance of Limbang. Rebel flags were flying from the Police Station and near-by buildings. In spite of atrocious weather conditions, Bridges managed to obtain more information than was available on his 1:253,440 scale map on which Limbang appeared as a red dot! Later the IO discovered some air photographs which, although taken in 1959, were quite useful.

Information as to the rebels' dispositions and strength was virtually non-existent. According to rumour the town was held by some thirty rebels. True or false, Bridges knew that speed was the important factor. His main aim was to release the hostages, unharmed, as soon as possible and he would have to use a simple plan with whatever force he had available when the time came.

Although 42 Commando had left Singapore by air and sea earlier, it soon became obvious that little of the Commando, except L Company, under Capt Moore, and part of the Support Company, would be available in time for the operation.

All that morning Lt Davis searched for suitable craft. He finally came up with two Ramp Cargo Lighters (RCLs) capable of transporting a company; but the craft were unarmoured and in less than peak condition. That afternoon the minesweepers *Fiskerton* and *Chawton* steamed up the Brunei River from Labuan with elements of L Company aboard. At once a working party from the ships' crews buckled down to make the RCLs shipshape. It was also arranged that the lighters would be manned by men from the minesweepers during the action against Limbang.

Moore did not know where the hostages were being held but decided that the most likely place was the Police Station—which would probably also house the rebel HQ. With the essence on speed once surprise had been lost, Moore decided to make a direct assault on the Police jetty, and to surround the Police Station at once.

At midday he had fifty-six men available; by 2000 the total had increased to eighty-nine. He was still one section short but this deficiency was filled by men from Company HQ. He also had under command one section of MMGs.

The Navy engineers worked throughout the day to ensure that both RCLs were serviceable and reliable. The only protection on the open decks, unfortunately, was one-and-one-half inch planking, varying in height from six to eighteen inches, so the Commandos used their large packs as sandbags. In order to minimize casualties in the initial assault, one craft was to land

Moore's Tactical HQ and 5 Troop opposite the Police Station. They would be covered from the second RCL by the remainder of the company and the MMGs. As soon as the Police Station was captured, the rest of the company would be landed and operations conducted according to information.

The attack was timed for first light of the 12th, but river navigation would be difficult in the extreme. The Limbang was tidal with many twists and turns and mud banks as it wound its way through the mangroves. The route lay through a complicated series of channels between fifty and a hundred yards wide. It was fortunate, considering these difficulties, that Captain Muton, the State Marine Officer, offered his services. He had already brought the minesweepers up the Brunei River earlier that day, and although he did not know the Limbang very well, his presence was bound to make a difference. In order to be certain of the timing for the assault, Moore decided to sail from Brunei at midnight and if necessary to lie up a wide channel before entering the main Limbang River around 0430.

At midnight the two lighters slipped into the muddy current of the river, manned by crews from *Fiskerton* and *Chawton*. A full moon helped Muton in his navigation as they chugged up-river. In spite of the leading craft losing one engine after an hour or so, and a few frightening but harmless arguments with *nipa* palms, the force reached the Limbang at about 0200 and lay up a side channel. At 0430 they came under way again, and about half an hour later the lights of Limbang appeared some distance ahead. One of the navigational difficulties had been the unknown strength of the current in the river, so their speed upstream could not be anticipated. As soon as Limbang came into view, Moore realized that they were too early and would arrive while it was still dark. He at once ordered speed to be reduced.

Shortly after 0500 the lights in Limbang suddenly went out. Moore at once suspected that his flotilla had been spotted, but decided not to increase speed. (It was never established if the switching off of the lights was deliberate or due to a fault; at any rate, there was no electricity during the next forty-eight hours.) Very slowly the RCLs approached the town. There did not appear to be any sign of life on the river side of the kampong to the north of the town. In fact, to the Marines crouching behind their packs, there was an ominous silence everywhere. But as the lighters rounded the bend leading to the Customs Wharf, the bazaar area—between the wharf and the Police Station—suddenly sprang to life. There was just enough light to see a large number of rebels running in all directions, very quickly disappearing into houses and behind cover. Some hundred yards further on, the Police Station was immediately recognizable, and the leading craft increased speed, making for the bank at a point about thirty yards upstream of it.

Sgt Smith, using a loud-hailer, announced that the rebellion was over, and called upon the insurgents to surrender. At once a machine gun hammered out from the Police Station, accompanied by rifle fire, the bullets sweeping across both lighters. Two Marines were killed in the leading craft and the Coxswain wounded; the company second-in-command and a seaman were wounded in the second. But both vessels continued on course, the Marines returning the fire from behind their packs, and the heavy chatter of the MMGs in the second craft neutralizing the Police Station until the leading lighter had closed the bank. Then the MMG Section switched its target zone northwards to the bazaar area.

As the assault craft beached, two sections of 5 Troop rushed ashore. Cpl Lester and his section doubled across the main road which separated the jetty from the Police Station, and through the rebel posts to the rear of the building. Sgt Bickford, the Troop Commander, with Cpl Rawlinson and his section pressed home a frontal attack. Rawlinson was wounded in the back, but continued to lead his men until the Police Station was captured.

Salleh bin Sambas, who had manned the rebel Bren gun, was wounded in the arm and chest, but he managed to withdraw from the building followed by the remnants of his force. Later he escaped on a bicycle with his brother. Three rebels were captured in the Police Station, though one tried to run away later and was shot.

Almost immediately after landing the first two sections, the lighter drifted off the jetty, probably because the Coxswain had been wounded. The Captain immediately took the wheel and brought her into the bank again near the District Office which was about three hundred yards upstream. Here, Sgt Macfarlane, accompanied by Sgt Smith who had decided that his loud-hailer was no longer a suitable weapon, led the reserve section ashore.

The Commandos moved north along the river bank towards the Police Station until they reached the hospital at roughly the half-way point. There were several rebels both around the buildings and in the jungle which reached down to within five yards of the rear of the hospital. In this very close country, Macfarlane cleared beyond the hospital while Smith searched the buildings.

Just north of the hospital a group of determined rebels were waiting in ambush for Macfarlane's section. The first burst of fire killed Macfarlane and two Marines, and wounded a third. The remainder of the Marines retaliated fiercely and the rebels fled into the jungle leaving several dead.

To the west of this ambush point, Smith was clearing the hospital buildings, a hand-grenade at the ready. He thought he heard movement inside and prepared to hurl the grenade when through the cracked windows came the sound of singing: 'They'll be wearing dark green bonnets. . . .'

Under the impact of his SL Rifle-barrel a window on the sheltered side of the room disintegrated. It was 0620 when Morris and his wife climbed out to safety.

Earlier, when the second-in-command was wounded in the opening fire of the operation, the CSM moved quickly to the bridge of the second RCL to take over the direction of the supporting fire, and to keep Command HQ informed of the progress on the rear link. During the early part of the fight, this craft was manoeuvred into the centre of the river to give the best supporting fire. Once the two leading sections of 5 Troop were established, and while the remainder of the troop were landing further upstream, the second craft was beached near the Police Station. The remaining Troops, 4 and 6, hurried ashore, then the lighter returned into midstream to give further MMG support. There were several rebels in a house about thirty yards up the hill behind the hospital and these were neutralized before the craft returned downstream and opposite the bazaar.

Meanwhile, 6 Troop cleared the area of the Police Station and 4 Troop moved up behind and north of it past the Mosque to the back of the town. A rebel gave 4 Troop some difficult and anxious moments by engaging them from a room full of women and children at the eastern end of a block of shops, but he was dislodged, and the troops entered the block.

Thereafter most of the rebel resistance collapsed, although a number of individuals held out in the town and in the jungle from where there was intermittent sniping for a further twenty-four hours.

By the afternoon the Commandos had formed a perimeter north through the hospital and Police Station to the first cross streets in the bazaar, and west and east from the river to the jungle. With night coming on fast, Moore decided to consolidate within this perimeter till the following morning. The MMGs had been landed, and during the morning the Assault Engineers and a section of mortars had arrived from Brunei as reinforcements.

As the Commandos' own medical officer was still in transit from Singapore, the MO from the 1/2nd Gurkhas had also come up with this party to take over from Sick Berth Attendant Clarke who had been collecting and caring for the casualties. The RCLs were returned to Brunei with the wounded Marines who were evacuated to Singapore the next day. Four of the six gunshot wounds had been in the legs; other casualties had been caused by men falling through the roof or floor of houses they were clearing.

During the night, the Marines patrolled beyond the perimeter to prevent the rebels from attempting to reorganize. On a number of occasions spasmodic rifle shots whined over the perimeter area from positions in the town further to the north. The Marines did not retaliate as the rebels could not be located accurately and there was the risk of causing injury to local inhabitants. In the jungle, which in places started right behind the buildings, it was a different story. Anything that moved was fired at, and in this way one rebel was killed. During the following day the remainder of the town was cleared.

In all, L Company lost five men. Fifteen rebels were found killed, and there were reports of a further twenty who died of their wounds later in the jungle. Salleh Kerrudin and Haji Pilok escaped, but the rebel commander was killed a few months later by a patrol from the 1/7th Gurkhas, and Haji Pilok surrendered in January.

A police constable, who had hidden in the roof of the Police

Station for five days without food or water, had heard the rebel leaders discussing the hostages on the evening of the 11th. They had, he said, decided to execute the hostages on the morning of the 12th. If L Company had arrived a few hours later it would have been too late.

Five miles south-east of Limbang lies the town of Bangar. At first light on the 14th M Company of 42 Commando moved upriver to Bangar in three miscellaneous craft manned once again by the crews from *Fiskerton* and *Chawton*. The twenty-six miles of difficult pilotage were achieved without incident, assisted by a Chinese—the only pilot available.

Probably due to their defeat at Limbang, the rebels had fled from Bangar after looting many shops, particularly food suppliers. As it seemed certain that the rebels were likely to try to escape eastwards, Bridges decided to move his HQ and K Company from Limbang to join M Company in Bangar.

The only armour in the territory at this time was provided by the Queen's Royal Irish Hussars. Two Ferret Scout Cars were to be ferried to Limbang in an old LCT to provide support for the Marines in clearing the Limbang–Bangar road. Unfortunately, because of a leaking ramp, the craft began to sink and was beached: the waterlogged Ferrets were no longer serviceable, but in the event the road was found to be clear of rebels. 42 Commando were now in the very heart of what later turned out to be the main 'hard-core' element of the rebels. From here the Commandos started to develop relentless pursuit operations which were to prove outstandingly successful.

FOUR
Regulars and Irregulars

When Mr Fisher, Resident of the Fourth Division, received the warning on the morning of 7 December, he not only passed it on to other interested parties, but it enabled him to take the necessary action to secure his own area. The Residency was at Miri, a coastal town about forty miles south-west of Seria. A few miles north of Miri was Lutong. Both these places were readily accessible only by sea or air.

Through the energetic measures taken by Fisher, his police, the staff of the Sarawak Shell Oilfields, and others, the rebels gained no footing in either Miri or Lutong. Bekenu, about twenty-five miles south-west of Miri, was taken over by the rebels, however, and an unknown number of Asian Government Officers held hostage. Twenty miles beyond Bekenu was Niah. Here, through the example and determination of two Survey Officers, the town was still in Government hands, but trouble was expected at any moment. Again both places were virtually approachable only by sea and then river, though infantry could advance slowly by jungle tracks.

The 1st Green Jackets, commanded by Lt-Col H. T. Sweeny, was on its way to Labuan in HMS *Tiger*. It soon became obvious that the considerable airlift to move the Green Jackets from Labuan could be avoided if *Tiger* was diverted to Miri. Fisher was warned to produce a Shell LCT and as many craft as possible for disembarkation by first light on the 12th, for the 10,000 ton cruiser would have to anchor some distance off shore.

The Resident collected the necessary craft and raised rather unwilling crews for the launches which were later to take the troops to Bekenu and Niah. It was a stroke of luck that these boats were available, because *Tiger* had landed the majority of her own boats before leaving Singapore in order to accommodate Army vehicles.

By 1030 on the 12th, the Green Jackets, less one company, disembarked with their stores. The remaining company was taken on by the cruiser to Labuan and subsequently flown to Seria for mopping-up operations between that town and Tutong.

At Miri, Sweeny was met by one of his officers who had arrived earlier by air and had made an aerial reconnaissance of Bekenu. This officer gave the colonel a description of the town and its approaches and without much delay the battalion moved into action.

At 1230 B Company, with two sections of the Sarawak Constabulary Field Force under command, sailed down the coast towards Bekenu in a Shell LCT towing two launches. The plan was for the company, less one platoon, to land on the coast at the nearest point adjacent to Bekenu. The force would then march overland to attack the rebels in the town, which was situated in the interior on the Sibuti River. Meanwhile, the remaining platoon would steam upriver in the launches to act as a cut-off. The Shell LCT reached the disembarkation point, but beached in eight feet of water, and the Green Jackets had considerable difficulty in getting ashore. The remaining platoon transhipped into one of the launches which then proceeded upriver towards Bekenu.

The main force, led by local guides, set off along the main track through dense jungle. The guides reported ambushes at two different places on the track, and long detours were made to avoid these. The going was extremely difficult as the troops sweated and cut their way through the jungle. By dawn of the 13th they had only reached the Sungei Dongales, still four miles from their objective. Local boats had to be obtained to cross the tributary, and luckily these were to hand, but only in sufficient quantity to take eight men at a time. The force was eventually carried over and by 0930 had closed to within four hundred yards of the rebel-held Government Building, Police Station and Chinese School. The platoon in the launch reported by radio that it was ten minutes away and as yet undetected.

The plan was for the Police Superintendent with the main force to call on the rebels to surrender, but before this could be done the rebels opened fire with shot-guns. The resistance had to be put down quickly because of the danger to hostages, and heavy return fire from the British troops soon accounted for six rebels killed and five taken prisoner. Twelve rebels managed to escape to Kampong Setap before the cut-off section was in position. Two platoons following up by launch captured eight of them and released a hostage. In Bekenu itself, two hostages were released. The Green Jackets suffered no casualties.

Earlier, before the attack, Sweeny had flown over the town and seen rebels on the roof of the Police Station jump to attention and salute as he flew past. Later he found out that according to rebel propaganda any aircraft with red fluorescent wing tips was Indonesian and friendly!

Later, C Company left Miri in a Shell LCT arriving in Niah by 1800. They found that the two Survey Officers had organized the villagers into a Home Guard, armed with shot-guns, to defend the place until their arrival. Although the houses along the river downstream from Niah were shut, the troops were enthusiastically welcomed in the village. One platoon occupied Niah, and another went further upriver to Rumah Pasang where a member of the Survey Team and Mrs Harrisson had organized a similar defence.

These irregular bodies of tribesmen grew to a strength of nearly two thousand and played a major role in blocking the rebel escape routes, and in providing an early warning screen in the event of any Indonesian infiltration. The irregular force owed its birth to Fisher who, on 9 December, summoned the tribesmen living along the Baram River to come to the assistance of the police in sealing off the rebels from the Miri-Lutong area. The organization was originally placed in the hands of Mr N. Coysh of the Sarawak Rubber Development Department. At least one hundred irregulars held the western end of the Baram and the ferry to stop the infiltration of rebels from Brunei. By the 11th more than one thousand loyal Kenyahs, Kayans, and Ibans had come down the river to Marudi, mostly armed with shot-guns. They were supplied with buckshot and rapidly deployed along the western border of Brunei to prevent rebel infiltration into the Fourth Division.

To link up with the Green Jackets' attack on Bekenu, Mr D. Reddish of Borneo Company and Mr J. Bagley of the Sarawak Medical Department, moved rapidly up the Bakong River recruiting many Ibans on the way. By the 14th this force, one hundred and twenty strong and divided into two large parties, had crossed the Sibuti watershed and was moving fast towards Bekenu. By using one route down the main Sibuti River, and a second across the headwaters of the Setap, they succeeded in sealing any escape inland after the attack on Bekenu.

Bagley's Force was reinforced by a company of Green Jackets in order to cut off the rebel retreat through the extensive farming area in the lower Setap. This successful tie-up of regular and irregular forces was only made possible by the extensive use of RAF aircraft for reconnaissance, and Royal Navy helicopters for the lift into positions.

The local population had allowed itself to be disarmed by the rebels and had been wavering in its loyalty, but the prompt arrival of Reddish's Force had an important psychological effect. The appearance of large irregular forces in the Sibuti area had a decisive effect on the adjacent inland tributaries of the Niah.

It was decided to place these irregulars under one command. The obvious choice was Tom Harrisson, who had an excellent knowledge of the country and the tribes, not only through his work as Curator of the Sarawak Museum, but also through his clandestine operations during the war against Japan. The river-based tribes were relatively easy to contact and command. The organization of the smaller, but tactically important elements in remote hill country, produced new problems involving landings by RAF Twin Pioneers and Belvedere helicopters. On one occasion, Harrisson was flown by 209 Squadron to an airstrip at Seridan, near the Indonesian frontier to make contact with the Laibits, a warlike tribe. Just to be on the safe side, the pilot of the Twin Pioneer buzzed the village to see if anyone fired on them. As they drew no fire the pilot landed, and Harrisson found the local people very friendly.

Wherever such landings could be made centres of armed resistance were established for the surrounding valleys. As its primary role, Harrisson's Force was deployed in a wide arc to block the escape routes of rebels within the coastal and sub-coastal areas. By the 15th all the possible escape routes had been closed. Although on a map it appears that there must have been countless escape routes, on the ground this was not so. North Central Borneo includes some of the most impenetrable terrain in South-east Asia. The number of practicable river-ways or

41

overland routes is small. Only the local people have a full knowledge of the complex geography—a knowledge which was at once utilized to keep watch on every route. Where the country was easier, larger-scale ambushes and patrols were mounted.

Many rebels tried to penetrate this screen, but few, if any, succeeded. The irregulars captured a hundred prisoners and quantities of arms and ammunition. More than three hundred of the irregulars had carried out para-military operations against the Japanese seventeen years earlier, and this had created several outstanding native leaders, who gave invaluable support to Harrisson and the small number of Britishers living in Sarawak. The rallying of the inland people also played a significant part in preventing those large sections of the sub-coastal population who were still undeclared from joining the rebels, for the spirit of aggressive determination generated from the inland tribes quickly spread outwards towards the coastal plain.

Within a week the Security Forces were in control of the situation in Brunei and Sarawak. The 1/2nd Gurkhas extended their authority over the whole triangle Brunei–Tutong–Muara. In Tutong, the inhabitants seemed frightened and sullen, and the Gurkhas had to rehabilitate the town. A force of rebels tried to infiltrate into Tutong during the night of 13 December in seven longboats but a Gurkha ambush accounted for twenty-six of them.

In the Limbang-Temburong Districts, which Brigadier Patterson had rightly predicted would be a hot spot for some time, 42 Commando continued to pursue the rebels. The Marines quickly gained control of the rivers Panduran, Temburong and Batu Apoi. Bases were established by helicopters and boats in several kampongs, and all rivers were patrolled by boats to impose a twenty-four hour curfew on river movement. F Troop 145 (Maiwand) Commando Battery, RA, was flown to Batong Duri to dominate the jungle further south with fire. By the 20th, two hundred and sixty-five rebels had been captured in the area, together with a large number of miscellaneous weapons including a Bren and fifteen rifles. But it was obvious that the final mopping up would take several weeks.

As a result of all operations in Brunei and Sarawak during the period 9 to 20 December, 40 rebels were killed, 1,897 were detained, and 1,500 'soft core' rebels were returned to their homes. The Security forces had suffered seven killed and twenty-eight wounded.

The revolt had totally disrupted the Brunei Government. The Sultan, his officials, and his advisers were not able to move into the Secretariat Building until the 10th. The effective resumption of civil government and administration was desperately slow, due partly to the necessity of the curfew during the early stages, and subsequently to the operational need of housing HQ 99 Gurkha Infantry Brigade in the Secretariat Building.

Perhaps the greatest impediment was the fact that many government servants had been implicated in the rebellion and were either in hiding or under detention. The Public Works and Marine Departments in particular were virtually stripped of every local employee. Little progress was made until the arrival of Mr P. H. Meadows on 18 December with the task of getting the civil administration back on its feet. On 20 December, the Sultan suspended the Sultanate's Constitution, dissolved the Legislative Council, and appointed a fourteen-man Emergency Council to hold power until the lifting of the Emergency. The Emergency Council was presided over by himself and consisted of four *ex-officio* members, including the British High Commissioner, Sir Denis White, and ten members nominated by the Sultan.

Although the revolt was confined to Brunei and Eastern Sarawak, there was for a time a feeling of uncertainty in other parts of Borneo. In West Sarawak, the Clandestine Communist Organization (CCO) did not take part in the rebellion, but were sympathetic to it. As a precaution the CCO leaders were arrested by the police, and the Communist Press was closed. To this internal danger was added the possibility of intervention by Sukarno.

On 14 December, 40 Commando, less one company, was landed at Kuching by HMS *Albion*. The same day Brigadier Barton, commanding 3 Commando Brigade, arrived in HMS *Blackpool* to act as the Governor's military adviser. The force came under Glennie's overall command, and he directed it to reconnoitre widely and make its presence felt in the three Divisions of West Sarawak, and to be in a position to assist the civil powers in restoring law and order if required. Various reports of infiltrations proved inaccurate, Sukarno still being unwilling to involve himself openly in the revolt.

The remaining area was North Borneo. For months past Naval presence had been periodically maintained in Tawau in conjunction with RAF Shackletons on anti-piracy patrols by air, sea, land, and river on the East Borneo coast. On 12 December, one of these patrols on the outskirts of Tawau discovered uniforms similar to those worn by the rebels in Brunei. Sir William Goode, Governor of North Borneo, at once asked Glennie to send a company to Tawau, but all troops were heavily involved in Brunei, and Glennie had to refuse. He did, however, send four Hunters which flew low over Tawau and Darvel Bay on the 15th, 16th, 17th and 19th. This was an effective way of showing that the Security Forces were alert to the situation, and it boosted local morale.

On the 16th, more rebel uniforms were found, and police intelligence sources indicated that the local Indonesian population of some 30,000 might create a disturbance. Consequently, B Company of the 1/2nd Gurkhas, then at Kuala Belait, was hurriedly flown to Tawau at 0400 on the 17th.

By the end of December the Brunei Revolt was virtually over; only the mopping up process continued. The swift arrival and bold use of troops and aircraft had thrown the TNKU organization into complete confusion. They were obviously unprepared for the fast build-up of forces and were soundly beaten in all major actions.

Unable to resist the Security Forces and disappointed at receiving no help from outside, the rebels had little choice but to surrender or flee. Some retreated into the interior intending to carry out terrorist activities from the jungle; others buried their arms and returned to their kampongs with the possible intent of causing fresh trouble once the Security Forces had relaxed their pressure.

But they were now in a difficult position. They were being driven into the jungle by troops with helicopters who could therefore move much faster than they, into territory off which they were unable to live on account of the hostility of the Irregular Forces. It is also important to note that most of the

5. Pilots had to be prepared to land anywhere. A helicopter from 845 Royal Naval Squadron descends in a small clearing.

6. Often a shingle bank was the only place to put down or take off troops.

7. Every forward base had its own helicopter pad—here a log platform.

rebels were coastal dwellers and accustomed to a life of comparative physical and psychological ease; they were not best suited to the rigours of jungle life. Now, disorganized, demoralized, badly armed and badly led, it was only a matter of time before they were all in the cage.

FIVE
Mopping Up

When the first shots of the Brunei Revolt were fired on 8 December, the man who was to play a major role in the destiny not only of Brunei, but of the whole of Malaysian Borneo, was some two thousand miles away in Nepal. Major-General Walter Walker, trekking through the remote areas of Nepal, partly in the performance of his duties as GOC 17th Gurkha Division, partly as a holiday, first heard the news on his ADC's transistor radio. He set out at once for the nearest aerodrome and managed to find a seat on a Dakota going to Singapore.

Walker is probably the greatest jungle fighter of the post-war period. He is also a man of considerable energy, insisting on hard and imaginative work from his officers and men. His Military Intelligence Officer once remarked: 'I used to be rather ashamed, as a much younger man, of feeling tired after a hard day flying with the General all over Borneo. He would visit various commands, making suggestions, listening to problems, then back to Headquarters for a cocktail party with local politicians to play his diplomatic role. He still would look remarkably fresh. And after the party, back to work with his light burning well into the early hours.'

On 19 December 1962, Walker assumed the duties of Commander British Forces in Borneo, replacing Brigadier Glennie who returned to Singapore as BGS/FARELF.

The command structure had originally been built on an *ad hoc* basis, but Walker now reorganized his forces at all levels, and at the same time established a first-class liaison with both police and civil administrations. While Walker's aim was to clear up the situation in Brunei as soon as possible he also kept a wary eye on the border with Indonesia, for he was certain that it would not be long before Sukarno made a move.

The mopping up in Brunei was, of necessity, a long job. Even with the use of helicopters, the area to search was vast and impenetrable, much of it swamp, criss-crossed with streams, and covered with thick jungle. To add to the difficulties the weather in the early part of January, 1963, was particularly vile. Heavy rain in the middle of the month unleashed the worst floods in living memory in the watershed of the Limbang river. At the peak of the floods the river had risen thirty feet and was, in parts, a mile wide. Houses and longhouses were submerged or swept away, the local population losing all it owned. By the 19th the floods had started to subside but there remained the problem of rehabilitating some 30,000 people in the Limbang area alone.

In March, General Walker said that the rebels still at large, 'will not be allowed to remain a running sore.' He was determined not to let the mopping up drag on for years as had the fight against the Communist Terrorists in Malaya. His aim, and promise, was to clear the Brunei jungles of rebels in time for the birth of *Malaysia* in August of that year.

The Security Forces continued their patrols, imposing a night curfew on Brunei Bay and River, making road and river checks, searching houses and kampongs. Several minor rebels were netted, but the leaders continued to remain at liberty. Yassin Affendi, and Azahari's brothers, Sheik Osman and Sheik Salleh, were still at large. Azahari himself had taken refuge in Indonesia. There was a price on Yassin Affendi of $(Malay) 15,000.

The importance placed by the Government and the Security Forces on the elimination of Affendi, coupled with their inability to capture him, gradually served to inflate his reputation to a ridiculous extent, creating a Robin Hood illusion which was far from the truth.

After the failure of the revolt Affendi, with about twenty men took to the vast mangrove swamps of Brunei Bay and East Sarawak. His intention was to stay hidden until the hunt was called off; perhaps he hoped that outside events would cause a quick withdrawal of the Security Forces to counter another threat. In any event the odds were heavily in his favour. At the end of March, his party left the Temburong swamps, crossed Brunei Bay, and established themselves in two groups. One,

47

about twelve strong and including Sheiks Osman and Salleh, hid out in a swamp north from the mouth of the Brunei. Affendi, with about five others, took to the swamp land bordering the river. In the first week of April, Azahari's brothers decided to leave their group, at least temporarily, and move to a more comfortable hideout near Brunei Town. Accompanied by one or two minor rebels, they came up the Brunei River hidden in the bottom of gravel boats and successfully pierced the security cordon. When the brothers reached Kampong Bunot, five miles from Brunei Town, they were given shelter in separate houses.

The Special Branch, however, had quickly learned of their arrival. Shortly before midnight, on 17 April, one of the houses was surrounded by a party from the 2/7th Gurkhas and the Special Branch.

The house was in complete darkness when a police officer climbed the steps and knocked at the front door. Voices were heard inside, the lights went on, and a man opened the door. The police entered and started searching the premises, but at that moment there was a burst from a Sterling machine gun. The lights went out, and someone shouted that a rebel was hidden in the roof. Four Gurkhas fired between the eaves and the ceiling. The Sterling stopped chattering abruptly, and a voice called out in Malay, 'I give up.' Then into the beam of a Landrover's head-lights came thirty-four year old Sheik Osman, covered in blood. He died a few days later.

The following day twenty-five year old Sheik Salleh, sick and anaemic, was also tracked down. He was armed with a .303 rifle, but wisely offered no resistance. Now only the elusive Yassin Affendi remained at large.

Early in April, General Walker made a tour of two battalions in the Limbang-Temburong District. While returning to Brunei by helicopter a message was received that Affendi was believed to be in the area of the airfield. At once the helicopter was diverted to assist in the search, and so for some minutes the General was personally engaged in the pursuit of his adversary. Although the Security Forces were not successful on that occasion, events were already moving towards the final episode in the swamp lands of the Brunei River.

During late April and early May, Gurkha troops and the Special Branch carried out numerous patrols which ultimately resulted in the arrest of two TNKU supporters and a village headman; these arrests led in turn to the surrender of three rebels two days later. One of these rebels said that he had previously hidden in a house near the mouth of the Brunei River. Willingly, he guided a patrol from the 2/7th Gurkhas to the house but it was empty. On further interrogation, the guide stated that he knew another man who might give a lead in to the chain of Affendi's supporters. After a long search, this second man was arrested on 14 May. Questioned for forty-eight hours, he finally gave the names of three food carriers. They were arrested on the 16th and handed over to the Special Branch.

By skilful interrogation the Special Branch obtained the name of yet another food supplier and arrested him on the 17th. This man admitted that he had taken food to a small party of rebels hidden in the swamp near Kampong Serdang, and said that he would guide the Security Forces to their camp. It was now late on the night of the 17th, and speed was essential because it would not be long before the rebels learned of the food supplier's arrest. Further, the rebel camp was accessible only at reasonably high tide, and in this respect conditions were likely to be favourable on the morning of the 18th.

Lt-Col A. N. Seagrim, commanding the 2/7th Gurkhas, decided that B Company would make the attack. Together with Special Branch officers and the arrested food supplier, Seagrim hurried to B Company Headquarters in two assault boats arriving at 0500 on the 18th. B Company, commanded by Major David Cutfield, was based on an island at the mouth of the Brunei River. Their task had been to deny the river to the rebels and to hunt down rebels in the mangrove swamps. Almost ninety per cent of their operations had been carried out from craft manned by the Assault Pioneer Platoon who achieved amazing proficiency in boatmanship and were accordingly known as 'Cutfield's Armada'.

On arrival at Company HQ, Seagrim quickly briefed Cutfield. The rebel camp was in the swamp on the north bank of the Brunei near Kampong Serdang, and about twenty minutes by canoe from the main river. Shortly after dawn, 'Cutfield's Armada' put to sea in their outboards. Within half-an-hour they had entered the Brunei River and were approaching the swamp which was over two thousand yards long and eight hundred yards wide. 6 Platoon was disembarked at the north-east extremity of the swamp, and 5 Platoon at the Serdang end. These two platoons established a line of cut-offs to block the escape routes to the landward side of the swamp while the Pioneer Platoon patrolled along the river edge of the swamp to prevent any escape by water.

At 0645 the assault party, consisting of Cutfield and ten Gurkhas, Captain Gregory of the Special Branch, his sergeant and the guide, entered the swamp in boats. They followed a small stream through the tangle of mangroves for about three hundred yards until the channel became too narrow and the boats had to be abandoned. The stream was too deep, so the party had to make its way forward by wading through the mud and mangroves. For one-and-a-half hours they squelched through the stinking, clinging mud, and stumbled over the arthritic mangrove roots, until it became apparent that the guide was not sure of his bearings. Cutfield led the way out of the swamp and walked down the bank to Serdang where he commandeered additional canoes.

At 0930 the assault group re-entered the swamp, this time travelling up a concealed stream in their canoes. The leading canoe carried the guide, Cutfield, Gregory, and the Special Branch sergeant. The other two carried the Gurkhas. They paddled upstream for about an hour and a quarter before the guide, now certain of his bearings, whispered that the rebel camp was about three minutes away. The first canoe load immediately disembarked and waded very slowly forward for about seventy-five yards. A towel was spotted through the mangrove screen and then the outline of a shelter. There was quite a lot of movement. Fearing that they had been seen, Cutfield at once opened fire in the direction of the movement, and the Special Branch sergeant called on the rebels to surrender. Abruptly, a rebel emerged from the mangrove, his hands raised, and said in English, 'It's all right, I won't run away.' He was Abdullah bin Jaffar, TNKU Area Commander of the district. He said that nine rebels had run away, and added that they were unarmed, which was untrue.

The Gurkhas now arrived at the camp and a follow-up started at once. The rebels had split into two groups, one going north, the other west. The tracks were easy to follow for there had been no previous movement by the rebels towards the mainland, so there were no old tracks to confuse the issue.

In the cut-off line beyond the swamp Rifleman Nainabahadur Rai waited patiently in a clump of overgrown rubber one hundred yards from his nearest comrade. He had been in this position for almost four hours; now the distant shots from the south warned him that the final stage of his patient vigil was approaching. A sudden movement caught his eye. Some seventy-five yards away through the tracery of rubber and undergrowth he sighted four rebels, but did not fire for fear of hitting his own men.

The rebels came nearer at a steady trot until the leading man, a pistol in his hand, saw Nainabahadur at about thirty yards' range. With a loud shout, the rebel and his three companions charged straight at the Gurkha. Coolly, Nainabahadur waited until the range halved before he fired. His first shot hit the leading rebel in the chest, passed through his body and hit the second rebel, killing them both. The others dropped to cover, but further shots from the rifleman wounded them both. He then closed in and took them prisoner.

The two who had been killed were top men of the Partai Ra'ayat. Of the two wounded, one was the TNKU Military Commander, Yassin Affendi himself. The other group of rebels were caught hiding in the undergrowth short of the cut-off line. One of these was Salleh bin Sambang who had led the rebels against Limbang. The tenth rebel surrendered on the following day. In their Regimental Journal, the 7th Gurkha Rifles summed up the result: 'The elimination of the TNKU command group was final and dramatic and after five months of tension, peaceful conditions had returned overnight to the waterways and kampongs of Brunei and East Sarawak.'

In Sarawak and North Borneo the events in Brunei were followed with great concern. The revolt was condemned by leaders of all political parties, and Azahari's claim to speak on behalf of the parties of the two territories was vehemently rejected. Even the Sarawak United People's Party, which was not in favour of Malaysia, condemned the activities of the TNKU.

Perhaps the most telling result of the revolt was that instead of gaining popular support among the peoples of Sarawak and

North Borneo, it led to a greater awareness among them of their common dangers and interests. In 1963 the local elections in North Borneo immediately after the revolt were fought on national issues, and resulted in an overwhelming victory for the pro-Malaysian candidates of the Sabah Alliance or associated parties. In the Sipitang District, where polling had to be postponed because of the revolt, elections were held in March, and in three other districts they were held in April. These results also showed wide support for Malaysia.

But the Sultan of Brunei still elected to stay out of Malaysia.

Part Two

CONFRONTATION

SIX
The Opening Gambit

In his book on guerrilla warfare, published in 1953, General Abdul Haris Nasution, Indonesia's former Defence Minister, states that both conventional and guerrilla warfare are total war. He stresses that guerrilla war is waged on all fronts: the military, the political, the socio-economic, the ideological, and the psychological. The inspiration for Nasution's theories was obviously provided by Mao Tse-tung, whose own writings on guerrilla warfare revolutionized its theory and practice, and General Vo Nguyen Giap, the brilliant North Vietnamese leader who crushed the French at Dien Bien Phu.

The Maoist theory of guerrilla warfare envisages a long-drawn-out struggle in three stages. During the first stage the guerrillas would be comparatively weak and content themselves with hit-and-run attacks on the enemy. During the second stage, the enemy's lines of communication would be stretched and he would tend to isolate himself in fixed bases. Guerrilla tactics would be to consolidate; attacks would be stepped up and the nucleus of a regular army would be built up for the third and final stage. In this stage, the enemy would be surrounded by a hostile population actively supporting the revolutionaries and under increasingly large-scale attacks, would become exhausted and demoralized to the point of annihilation or submission.

Even before Dien Bien Phu, Nasution wrote, 'The war in Indo-China has proved that persevering guerrilla fighters can raise their army to the division level and that even though its equipment was not very modern compared with that of the enemy, by using guerrilla warfare and supported by a burning spirit they could gradually change from the defensive to the offensive, in spite of the fact that the enemy had complete control of the air.'

A fundamental axiom of Maoist thought is that guerrilla

55

campaigns are revolutionary movements. The defeat of the French in Indo-China was due largely to their inability to cope with a revolutionary situation. Similarly, many of the errors of judgement in the subsequent campaign against the Vietcong were due to the failure to grasp the revolutionary, political nature of the Vietcong movement. One of the commonest errors in dealing with such a situation is to overestimate the value of sophisticated equipment and superior fire-power. The importance of political action is paramount. Guerrilla war in the Malay Archipelago, as in Vietnam, was total war and it demanded new and unconventional tactics.

With the failure of the Brunei Revolt, Sukarno had to make a more direct move in his plan to 'crush Malaysia!' His main policy from the beginning was to divide the various states, break up the conception of unity, and bring Malaya and Singapore under a government subservient to Indonesia. His first object was to separate Sarawak and North Borneo from Malaysia using tactics based on Nasution's theories of guerrilla warfare. He would alternate military and political pressures, before switching to simultaneous military and political pressure. After raising the political pressure until Malaysia reacted, he would then lower it to the accompaniment of loud protestations of his 'peaceful' intent.

Eastern Malaysia, the battleground of what became known as 'Confrontation', comprises Sarawak (47,000 sq miles) and Sabah (29,000 sq miles) on the north and north-western side of Borneo—the third largest island in the world. For administrative purposes, Sarawak is broken up into five Divisions, each in turn sub-divided into Districts. Sabah (originally called North Borneo until becoming part of Malaysia) is administratively divided into four Residencies.

The coastline of Malaysian Borneo, including Brunei, stretches for 1,500 miles, and the land frontier with Indonesian Borneo (Kalimantan) is almost 1,000 miles long, the distance from Liverpool to Warsaw.

The country is a vast roadless, rail-less expanse of jungle and mountain. The main lines of communication to Borneo are by sea and air. The numerous rivers and a few jungle trails are the only means of travel between coast and hinterland, a factor which has accounted for the low level of internal development in the area. The largest and most developed centres of population lie along the coast and are bordered by low-lying plains, punctuated by small hills. The lowlands are mostly swampy and in a few places the hills reach the sea, forming sea-cut cliffs. In some coastal areas there is a narrow strip of forest on raised dry land termed beach woodland. On the muddy shores and river estuaries, where there is flooding at high tide, are dense mangrove swamps. In non-tidal fresh-water swamps, the trees are not tall but there is extensive undergrowth.

Between the coast and the mountainous border country, much of Borneo is covered by dense, tropical rain forest which forms an almost unbroken canopy a hundred feet or so above the ground. During Confrontation, hand beacons were often used by the troops as a homing device. If a soldier lost sight of the back of the man immediately in front of him, the odds were ten to one that he would lose his way and get separated from his group.

The Sarawak border with Kalimantan, running from the west, rises rapidly to three thousand feet and culminates in mountains rising to eight thousand feet. The Sabah border continues on at eight thousand feet, and gradually descends to three thousand. Sections of relatively level land are interspersed amongst the ranges and these are settled and cultivated by hill tribes.

As there are no roads or railways, transport in the area is mainly waterborne, leading to a coastal and river civilization. Most of the population live within easy reach of waterways. The population is a conglomeration of many races: Malays, the indigenous tribes—Ibans, Muruts, Kelabits, Kayans, Punans, and many others, and Chinese, the largest immigrant population and potentially the gravest threat to internal security in Eastern Malaysia.

Even before the capture of Affendi, which finally wound up the Brunei Revolt, Sukarno had launched his long-expected guerrilla attack against Sarawak. In the early hours of Good Friday, 12 April, 1963, some thirty Indonesian raiders penetrated three miles into the First Division, and attacked the police post at Tebedu. Under cover of darkness, they crawled through an open drain which ran beneath the ten-foot high link fence surrounding the post, and took the small police detachment completely by surprise. In the Charge Room a corporal was killed when trying to raise the alarm. In the near-by sleeping quarters two more policemen were wounded. The sudden shots awoke Inspector Chimbon, the post commander. Rushing from his quarters he engaged the enemy, but the heavy return fire forced him to take cover in a water tank. The raiders then made their way through the bazaar, looting watches, jewellery, transistors, and cloth but, surprisingly, no foodstuffs.

At this time the Commander Military Forces, West Sarawak, was Lt-Col J. M. Strawson of the Queen's Royal Irish Hussars. His command consisted of C Squadron, QRIH, and B Company, 40 Commando. The Commando were deployed in three areas: HQ and one troop at Kuching, and one troop each at Bau and Serian. Word of the raid reached Strawson at 0400, and he at once ordered the Commandos to investigate the situation. 6 Troop, under Lt Douglas Keelan, was dispatched in the Hussars' Landrovers to organize the local Home Guard and arrange defences. The road passed through very rough country, and the thirty mile drive took three hours.

One of General Walker's Staff Officers telephoned him at dawn. 'Tebedu Police Post has been captured, sir, and all the police taken prisoner.' First reports in this type of campaign are often inaccurate and make the situation seem a lot worse than it really is. The General was fully committed at the time to a big hunt for Affendi. His only reserve was B Company, King's Own Yorkshire Light Infantry, but he decided to take a calculated risk and send it to Sarawak. The company was in the jungle, and an Auster was flown to the area to summon the troops by loud-hailer to a rendezvous on a main track.

Walker also decided to send 846 Royal Naval Squadron to Kuching, but the Staff Officer told him that the squadron was carrying out aircraft maintenance, and in fact one helicopter's engine had been removed for a check.

'How long will the squadron take to get operational?' asked Walker.

'It will take a week, sir.'

'Make it a night,' said Walker.

Undeterred, the Naval ground crews did a quick change and all six Whirlwinds flew down to Kuching the next day, deliberately flying over the town in display formation to boost morale.

In January, 3 Commando Brigade Group, commanded by

Brigadier Barton, had withdrawn to Malaya from West Sarawak although it was known that should conditions deteriorate they would have to return. Indeed, in February the joint planning staff of the C-in-C Far East had begun preparing contingency plans to meet this very possibility.

Simultaneous with the attack on Tebedu Police Station another danger came to light. The Special Branch revealed an alarming and hitherto unsuspected degree of preparedness by the Clandestine Communist Organization within West Sarawak. Large quantities of Chinese weapon-training pamphlets had been discovered. Captured suspects revealed that practical training within the organization had advanced to the stage of rehearsals for raids on police stations, ambushes, and other forms of militant action.

On Saturday 13 April, the Sarawak Emergency Committee decided that military assistance was urgently needed to help the police in confiscating over 8,500 shot-guns, mainly Chinese-owned, which were on the police register. That evening 3 Commando Brigade HQ and 40 Commando in Malaya, began to recall all ranks. But it was Easter Saturday and officers and men were scattered throughout the Peninsula. Nevertheless by Easter Sunday a team headed by General Wyldbore-Smith, the Chief of Staff to the C-in-C, Far East Command, and including Barton, flew to Kuching to make an on-the-spot assessment.

Barton remained in Kuching, and that afternoon C Company of 40 Commando was flown in from Singapore. The following morning Tactical HQ arrived and was quickly followed by the bulk of 40 Commando.

Meanwhile, *Albion* had sailed for Sarawak with the remainder of 40 Commando and the 2/10th Gurkha Rifles. The Commandos were disembarked at Kuching, and the Gurkhas were transferred, off the mouth of the Rajang river, to smaller craft which ferried them upriver to Sibu.

Operation Parrot started at dawn on 19 April. It was primarily a police operation with the military standing by in case of trouble. The whole operation was handled very smoothly; on the first day over six hundred and fifty shot-guns were handed in at police centres in the First and Second Divisions. In the Third Division, where CCO activity was more hardened, the police thought it would be prudent to search some of the suspected houses in Sibu before the shot-gun withdrawal was announced. With military support, the result was much better than the police had hoped. Twenty shot-guns were recovered, and four CCO youths were captured doing PT in the middle of the night. An unexpected bonus was an opium pipe and some opium which were thrown from the back window of a house on stilts straight into the hands of a startled Gurkha rifleman standing up to his waist in water!

By the end of the first week nearly 8,000 of the 8,514 registered shot-guns had been handed in. There appears little doubt that the authorities were one jump ahead of the rebels but the confiscation of shot-guns was only the first phase; soon the emphasis began to swing to increased patrolling. It was decided to retain a small tactical HQ and two rifle companies of the 2/10th in the Second Division, together with a troop from C Squadron, QRIH. The remainder of the 2/10th was responsible for security in the Third Division. In the First Division were 40 Commando, Lloyd's Company and L Company of 42 Commando, B Company KOYLI, and C Squadron QRIH less, of course, the one troop in Second Division.

Brigadier Barton was Commander of British Forces in West Sarawak, and in overall command of operations was General Walker, while in Singapore Admiral Sir Varyl Begg had taken over as Commander-in-Chief of British Forces in the Far East.

At the time of the Tebedu raid, the Indonesians had left behind documents intended to give the impression that the operation had been carried out by TNKU volunteers and was an offshoot of the Brunei Revolt. But it was apparent from later evidence that this first raid had, in fact, been carried out by Indonesian regular soldiers, probably to ensure its success.

During the early stages of Confrontation the Indonesian raiders consisted, for the most part, of 'volunteers', led and trained by the cream of Sukarno's Army: Marine Commandos (KKO), Army Paratroopers (RPKAD) and Air Force Paratroops (PGT). The men of these specialized regular units had to undergo extremely tough training and were able to exist with the minimum of administrative backing. As leaders of Indonesian Border Terrorist (IBT) units, they slowly moulded a mixture of volunteers from all races into something approaching passable military standards. The volunteers were a mixed bunch: Menados, Javanese, Malayan, and some from native Borneo tribes. Their military backgrounds were as varied. Many had served in West Irian, Celebes, and against the Dutch in the struggle for independence; some were stragglers from the Brunei Revolt. There were others who 'volunteered' for service after being convicted for barter-trading, smuggling or piracy. Their training was sketchy, but they all came from peasant families and for the most part were accustomed to living in the jungle and surviving on the minimum of rations.

In the early hours of 23 April, 1963, about fifteen of these volunteers opened fire on the police post at Gumbang which was only two hundred yards inside the border of the First Division. The post had been reinforced by a half section from C Company of 40 Commando. They at once returned the fire, aiming at the flashes of the raiders' guns. One Marine was slightly wounded in the arm, but two of the IBTs were killed and three wounded. At dawn, blood trails were found leading over the border. As at Tebedu, documents were left behind to indicate that the raid had been led by a lieutenant of the TNKU.

Four nights later at Tebedu, while the sentries were being changed, two or three raiders crawled to within twenty yards of the position, cut the alarm system—laying them to one side—and removed the *panjis* (sharpened bamboo stakes). They then kept firing with a shot-gun and an LMG for five minutes. The Commandos returned the fire, and the attackers retreated. A follow-up revealed nothing. Tracker dogs were rushed to the scene but the scent was too weak. The raid had been a timid hit-and-run affair, but had obviously been carried out by men trained in fieldcraft.

The long, ill-defined jungle-covered border between Sarawak and Kalimantan, with its numerous established crossing places, called 'gates', proved easy entry and departure points for the raiders. It was clear that control of the border by the Security Forces must be given top priority. At this early stage, attacks were aimed at isolated posts where the raiders hoped to capture arms and ammunition. To counter this, Barton established forts near the border to be used as patrol bases; they were made up to platoon strength and situated in existing kampongs and bazaars. Sappers constructed defence works and helicopter LZs at these forts. A curfew over an area some five miles deep was imposed between 2000 and 0400 along the border in the First and Second Divisions. Ambushes were laid, and during the curfew period fire could be opened without warning. Half of 845 Squadron and all of 846 were at Kuching to give support and deploy patrols along the border in order to react quickly to enemy raids.

For three weeks the situation remained quiet, then on 17 May the Indonesians struck again. This time they chose a civilian target. Two Ibans and a Chinese trader lived in some boats at Nangga San in the Second Division. About thirteen armed bandits knocked on the door of the two hawker boats, and after calling on the occupants to let them in, opened fire with an automatic and rifles. The three locals dived into the river, one suffering a slight bullet graze on his bottom. The raiders then made off with about $(Malay)2,000 worth of goods.

The IBTs' purpose, while outwardly looting, was clearly aimed at establishing their identity as armed forces capable of crossing the border when necessary in support of an internal insurrection. This change in tactics increased the Security Forces' problems enormously. More troops would be needed if the attacks were no longer to be confined to military posts. Lt-Col Fillingham, commanding 2/10th Gurkhas, made strong representations for the move of the rest of his battalion to the Second Division. This was agreed, and the Third Division was taken over by the 1/10th Gurkhas.

Two subsequent incidents of armed raiders intimidating civilians caused Fillingham to move C Company further east so that the battalion could cover the area right up to the boundary between the Second and Third Divisions, boosting his force with the Pioneer and Reconnaissance Platoons. In this way he was able to cover nearly every track over the boundary with small ambush parties; at one stage there were twenty-nine permanent ambushes along the 120 miles of the Second Division border.

The problem was to prevent the locals from crossing the border and stumbling into the ambushes. Many of the local people had relatives in Kalimantan and considerable trading was also carried on; with many commodities in short supply on the

Indonesian side, both Governments had turned a blind eye to the practice. Now the situation was different, but it took a long time for the order to reach longhouses, nor was it always observed.

By far the biggest problem was the difficulty in distinguishing friend from foe. Many local Ibans owned shot-guns, and carried them whenever they left the longhouse. They dressed in an assortment of civilian clothes and military uniforms. The IBTs wore a similar motley garb—so the lot of the young NCO or rifleman in an ambush position was hardly enviable. Should an innocent Iban be killed accidentally the local population and the civil government would react strongly; if, on the other hand, an armed enemy was allowed to slip through, higher command would react equally strongly!

During this period the helicopter came to play an increasingly important role in the operations. On one occasion a fort on the border forty miles away was reinforced with ten men in twenty-five minutes. Normally this would have taken ten hours—including a seven-hour trek.

Because of the value of dogs as trackers, and to give warning of ambushes, volunteers from both Commando units took a course in dog-handling. The first five dog-handlers passed out on 1 June 1963, and from then on ambush dogs worked with many of the border outposts.

The gradual establishment of the Security Forces changed the CCO policy. The young Chinese who were prepared to volunteer for military training in the organization were severely handicapped by Security Force patrolling in their training areas. They were forced to move in small groups across the border into Kalimantan. Each group was told they would do two months' training, then return to await an internal uprising.

On 7 June, fifty-four young Chinese of both sexes were arrested while waiting in the forest to meet a guide who was to take them over the border, an indication of the extent to which the Chinese were defecting into Kalimantan. It was estimated that some six hundred and fifty defected during that period. The Indonesian authorities, however, were anxious to deny that the CCO was engaged in Confrontation. Training and equipping a militant Chinese organization was not consistent with Indonesian propaganda claims that Malaysia was in danger of being taken over by Chinese Communists, and that Sukarno's opposition to Malaysia was an attempt to prevent an outpost of Peking being established in South-east Asia.

There is no doubt that the Indonesians found the young Chinese very useful. Some were already indoctrinated in the theory of guerrilla warfare. Whatever the long-term consequences, help for the CCO would have a disruptive effect on Sarawak. In spite of this, there was a tendency on the part of the Indonesians to treat their Chinese allies with disdain.

Near the border, the Indonesians continued to make terrorist raids, attacking a longhouse and a shop in the first week of June. One party of raiders met a lone Gurkha sergeant who was reconnoitring an ambush position. His sub-machine-gun unfortunately jammed and he was shot in the head. The raiders departed with the gun.

With the increase in terrorist raids, the Security Forces had to change their plans by attempting to catch the enemy at the location of the raid rather than on the border. It was not long before the Indonesians received two bloody noses.

Towards the end of June, Fillingham received information that a party of IBTs had arrived in Mawang, opposite the Second Division. The same gang had made the previous raids, and the Gurkhas hastily prepared to meet them. As soon as the gang crossed the border helicopters were used to establish cut-off parties, and the hunt was on. The rebels were quickly caught by the Gurkhas, and suffered three killed and two wounded. Among the weapons captured after the fight were the SMG seized from the Gurkha sergeant, and a No. 5 rifle the rebels had taken from Tebedu. One of the dead bandits was the headmaster of a Roman Catholic School at Mawang who had joined the TNKU the previous year.

A few days later another patrol made contact. Unfortunately it was only just past 2000 and, as curfew had barely begun, the section commander had to challenge the men approaching his ambush position. The bandits rushed for cover, but one was killed and his Sten gun captured.

In the enemy camp, overall direction in Borneo was placed under the Indonesian Army, while Malaya came under Navy control. A number of encircling frontline bases were to be built up in the Rhio Islands and Sumatra, overlooking Singapore and the Peninsula, on which stores and explosives could accumulate and from which attacks could later be launched.

Meantime, the agents already infiltrated into Malaya and Singapore were instructed to obtain defence secrets, use explosives to create terror and weaken the power of resistance to future attack, and find suitable beaches for naval landings. Bogus shipping companies were formed to provide communication links and employment for the agents. Malay political parties were encouraged to engage in repressive anti-Chinese measures. The Indonesian Navy was instructed to terrorize Malay fishermen.

Meanwhile, training continued in Sumatra. A camp was formed at Tanjong Sekupang. From there recruits could see the lights of Singapore. In addition to conventional military training, they were taught how to blow up bridges, power stations, railway lines, public buildings, and water reservoirs. Political indoctrination was continuous. After completing their training they infiltrated into Singapore with orders to create chaos and terror. A number of incidents took place. Large gatherings, clubs, and public utilities were chosen as targets, and the explosions were intended to show the world that there was no peace in Singapore.

From early December, 1963, the smuggling of explosives increased, while arms and ammunition were added to the steadily increasing 'imports'. The Singapore police were very active and arrested many Indonesian agents and gun-runners, including fourteen former West Irian volunteers, eleven PMU members, and five former employees of the Indonesian Consulate.

Although the Indonesian agents' first attempts were clumsy and amateurish, the Special Branch was aware that improved training would soon lead to serious acts of sabotage. They anticipated a long, hard task in defeating Sukarno's Fifth Column.

SEVEN
'One Thousand Pairs of Eyes'

One of the most important recipes for success in a war against guerrillas is timely and accurate information. General Walker was well aware of this, and was determined to have a first-class Special Branch and Military Intelligence machine.

Unfortunately, the incubating Malaysia was unprepared for the emergency. With the formation of Malaysia, the system of central government directed from Kuala Lumpur was in a transitional stage and as yet untried in Sarawak and Sabah. A wide sea separated eastern Malaysia from Kuala Lumpur and from the HQ of the C-in-C FARELF at Singapore.

Both Sarawak and Sabah had been peaceful, law-abiding countries with practically no crime. The combined police forces numbered less than the police in one small state on the mainland. Only in three places along the 1,000 mile border were there police posts close to the frontier. The bulk were on the coast and in the main towns. There was no locally-raised navy or army, just a small Maritime Police Force.

The more serious shortage was in the Special Branch. Walker was a strong supporter of the Special Branch in the field of intelligence, for the simple reason that police officers and their staff and agents lived in the country, spoke the language, knew the people—indeed, were of the people. The army intelligence staff, by contrast, was constantly changing, even though reliable intelligence demands continuity at every level. The expansion of the Special Branch was therefore given immediate priority. There was already an excellent nucleus to build on as proved by Operation Parrot. Walker also realized the importance of liaison between the Military and Civil. His clear understanding of the necessity for the closest partnership between military and police in operations of this kind led to excellent relations between the two forces.

66

The main source of military intelligence was very reliable indeed—the 22nd Special Air Service Regiment, commanded by Lt-Col John Woodhouse, and subsequently by Lt-Col Wingate Gray. The primary task of the SAS was to provide an early-warning system. In the jungle, where the Indonesian raiders could slip across the border unobserved, it was necessary to have mobile observation points, but because of the vast distances involved and the nature of the country, conventionally trained troops could not be used. Small detachments of the SAS, often less than half-a-dozen, would be taken by helicopter and dropped in the jungle where they would remain for weeks on end. The men had to be tough and extremely well-trained. As a rule they did not attack the enemy; their main task was to radio back information and leave it to the infantry to mop up the invaders. But sometimes they had no option, and although nearly always outnumbered, gave ample proof that they could look after themselves.

Walker had considerable respect for the SAS and their capabilities. He said: 'I regard 70 troopers of the SAS as being as valuable to me as 700 infantry in the role of Hearts and Minds, border surveillance, early warning, stay behind, and eyes and ears with a sting.'

A third and unique intelligence source was initiated by Mr Fisher, Resident of the Fourth Division, and Walker's brother-in-law. The use of Harrisson's irregular force in the later stages of the Brunei Revolt had brought the whole problem of border surveillance into focus. Fisher convinced the General that a force could be raised of 'one thousand pairs of eyes and ears', but Walker suffered innumerable frustrations at all levels of government, police, and GHQ before he was able to persuade Sarawak to raise the Border Scouts. The Sarawak Government had to sell some shares to finance the project, and an order was promulgated on 10 May 1963. Sabah waited almost until Merdeka Day to make similar arrangements. The Sarawak Constabulary, helped by Major T. Leask of 22 SAS, Mr Tom Harrisson, a representative from the Commandos, and the Archdeacon of Kuching set to work to hammer out a charter to launch this valuable indigenous force. Apart from the difficulties of organization, equipment, and command, there was the problem of starting anything during the twilight period which marked the end of colonial rule in Sarawak. All major decisions were put off until Independence was declared.

A force of this nature required a commander with unusual talents and with experience in dealing with indigenous tribes. Walker decided that Major John Cross was the man for the job. He had already proved himself in the Malayan jungle during the Emergency. Walker impressed on Cross that if civilian morale broke down Confrontation would succeed. If the Border Scouts were effective, however, civilian morale would not break down, and Confrontation would fail. 'That is why I called you to take on this post,' Walker concluded. 'Now get on with it.'

Unfortunately Cross was not present when the Border Scouts were first raised. The whole object of having Border Scouts was to employ them in a, so-to-speak, 'bare-arsed' role, working on the border in their civilian clothes, which often consisted of little more than a loin cloth, bringing back information from places where the Security Forces could not go without being recognized. The first recruits were formed as military units and given a sketchy three weeks' training in minor tactics and weapon-handling under the supervision of the SAS and the Gurkha Independent Parachute Company. Many of the early recruits were the wrong type of men, and the Scouts developed into rather poor militia. It is a common misconception that Borneo is populated by the 'brave Iban' who will chop off anybody's head as a matter of course. Certainly the largest group of indigenous tribes is Iban, but by no means all of these colourful, mercurial and earthy people are fierce.

Along the border at least thirty different languages are spoken, some merely dialectal, others totally distinctive. Five main languages are spoken in the First Division alone, not counting Malay, English, or any Chinese dialect. Between the two extremities of Borneo there is as great a diversity of language, climate, habit, dress, religion, and custom as is found between Ireland and Italy. Cross described the border as, 'A cartographer's folly. The result of a package deal between two colonial powers with as much or as little importance or concern as anyone wanted to invest in it. The border had, until recently, as much significance to most natives as a child in England going to school across the parish boundary would have to its parents.'

Cross did a lightning tour of Sarawak, giving priority to the

First and Second Divisions. He started to retrain and re-organize the Border Scouts. From the beginning, NCOs of the Gurkha Independent Parachute Company had been placed in charge of sections and they remained as section commanders of newly formed and trained sections.

The status symbols of uniform and rifle having been given to the Scouts, a complete return to the original conception could not be achieved overnight. In much of the area troops were short on the ground, and at first it had seemed an excellent idea to use the native Scouts as satellites to remote longhouses, but it was soon to prove an unhappy situation. Except for the fact that the use of the Scouts in this way identified border kampongs and longhouses with the task of defending their own country and kin, their suitability for employment in static defensive positions was limited. Within a few months the incident at Long Jawai was to prove this point in a dramatic and tragic fashion.

For the lone Gurkha in charge of his Border Scout section, miles from anywhere, and with the difficulty in language, the life was lonely and strange. His charges were frightened by the possibility of a fight, and were unused to Gurkha discipline. In the early days the Gurkha did not fully trust his men, and during a four-day ambush would not normally take off his boots or go to sleep during the entire time. But for the most part the Gurkha NCOs were steadfast and achieved as favourable results as the circumstances would allow.

It was obvious, however, that the Border Scouts should have their own leaders. Patient and sound training by Gurkha Officers and NCOs produced highly successful results and locally-promoted corporals were eventually leading their own sections.

But the 'bare-arsed' role was the most important part the Scouts had to play, and Cross worked hard to achieve this. For seven months he rarely spent more than a day or two in one place, and with hardly any time off to relax. By early 1965 he had to resign. 'It was either that or an early grave.' He had, however, achieved his aim. Besides the uniformed Scouts who guarded longhouses and accompanied Security Forces on patrols as guides, more and more were employed as the eyes and ears of the intelligence system. Eventually their duties included scout-ing, surveillance of border crossing places, examination of and reporting on tracks, guides to military parties, local defence of kampongs where there were no military, and above all getting information back to the local company commander.

Although at their best the Scouts were very good indeed, they had their limitations. Some were in it only for the pay and had to be chased into activity. But by and large, with their vast knowledge of the border area, they proved a valuable source of intelligence.

The badge devised for the uniformed Scouts was a Hornbill, worn on the left arm. Before his departure, Cross put new words to the *Scarlet Pimpernel* jingle:

> He wanders here, he wanders there,
> The Hornbill wanders everywhere,
> So seldom in, so often out,
> That damned elusive Border Scout.

EIGHT
'Hearts and Minds'

No guerrilla operations are possible without the full co-operation of the local people. This was apparent at the time of the Malayan Emergency, when General Templer coined the phrase, 'Hearts and Minds'. The principle applied even more in Borneo, and Walker emphasized its importance to all his commanders. It was as much a battalion commander's task to win over the local people as it was to achieve results in actual fighting against a heavily-armed enemy. By winning over the people, he could assure that the enemy would be isolated from supplies, shelter, and intelligence.

The old system of giving salt, tobacco, sugar, and beads was wrong for Borneo. Tact, courtesy and, above all, infinite patience and human understanding were needed. It was the responsibility of all ranks to establish good relations, and this was done to a high degree by all troops in the area. Bartering of a minor nature continued non-stop; and in this respect the character of British and Gurkha troops readily lends itself to conforming with local behaviour. It was also important to uphold at all times the dignity and prestige of the local headman. One way of accomplishing this was by allowing him to take the salute at 'Retreat'!

Like all primitives, the locals believed that the Army was omnipotent and so thought it quite fair to demand help at all times. They made endless requests for trips to outlying kampongs, movement of rice, planks, children, old people and pigs by helicopter. Because of personnel changes involving airlifts and weekly ration drops helicopters were frequently flying around forward areas, and the locals came to rely more on the soldiers and airmen than on the civil administration, a practice further encouraged by the fact that medical orderlies were

71

always present with the companies. This threw a heavy, sometimes excessive, load on the local commander who had to weigh the urgency of requests and decide priorities. There was also the danger that when the soldiers departed a vacuum would be left which might in the long run be detrimental to the natives.

The longhouse is synonymous with Borneo. A longhouse is a village within a village. Built on stilts and invariably beside a river, the building is divided into three main parts. Outside there is a veranda which faces the river and is the highest part of the house. It is used for drying clothes, and more often than not the bamboo floor is rotten. Inside is a long, central corridor, which is the main street, debating ground, dance floor, and many other things. Here you will find fighting cocks, and the house dogs who are kicked, abused and trodden on.

The longhouse contains from twelve to sixty families, each having its own room and a door onto the central corridor. The wealth of the family is measured by the number of gongs and earthenware pots they possess—the pots hold rice and *tuak* (rice wine), and are never allowed to become empty. The walls are of bare wood and adorned with pictures of the Royal Family. The floors are slatted bamboo which simplifies the plumbing and sanitation problems. Under the house are the pigs who keep it fairly free of filth. Access is up a notched ladder. There are attics which contain stores, mats, and baskets, and where women prepare the rice and corn. Outside the headman's door hang the ceremonial shields, swords and spears of the house. There are dusty, blackened skulls of victims, a few of whom were Japanese, but the majority are relics of the nineteenth century. In the old days the Iban warrior had to bring a head to his bride before he could claim her in marriage. The usual method was to wait in ambush for some unsuspecting person, and dispatch him with a poisoned dart from a blow-pipe.

The basic food is rice, flavoured with jungle pig, fish, and various types of jungle food such as bamboo shoots, prickly palm ferns and mushrooms. The food is served to the men, on plates set in a circle on bamboo mats on the floor, by the women, who also do the cooking. The older women go bare-breasted, but many of the younger girls are becoming more 'civilized' and wear transparent silk blouses with bras. Shoes are never worn in the house.

72

The Johnson 40 h.p. outboard is as much a status symbol as the skulls of victims in past days. This has been more recently superseded by the helicopter pad—some of the young Ibans have added a helicopter design to the customary tattooing on their bodies.

The Iban loves a party, and this is one way in which the Security Forces were able to make contact and establish friendly relations. The party usually starts with an offering to the Gods —a *Bersadang*. The senior guest waves a live chicken over seven bowls (of rice, betel nuts, tobacco, and sireh leaves among other things) completing each revolution with the hope that the Pengulu (headman) enjoys good health, long life, crops, good omens next year, and anything else he can think of. The Ibans sit in a circle and approve each declaration. If the guest is particularly important he will get a *Pantun*, or song of welcome.

Once the preliminaries have been completed, serious drinking begins, while the dancers perform. Dressed in hornbill head-dresses, and waving parangs, the dancers emphasize the martial attributes of the Iban warrior to the beating of gongs, the tempo growing more furious as the evening progresses. The guests are also asked to dance, and as long as it is something simple, like twisting, the hosts are well pleased. Eventually everyone staggers to bed and at the crack of dawn are awakened by the unbelievable noise of all the fighting cocks crowing in unison.

Gradually the Security Forces began to establish friendly relations with the locals. When the forward companies held sick parade, the villagers also turned out. Among the local Muruts, Lt Pancharaj Rai of the 2/7th Gurkhas won considerable acclaim as a doctor even though his remedy for all ailments from toothache to boils was two paludrine tablets!

There were, of course, many occasions when the Security Forces were able to help in cases of real emergency. When a cholera epidemic struck the Ibans in 1964, 845 Squadron flew some two hundred Ibans to hospital, many at night from dangerous jungle LZs. On the ground sick berth attendants inoculated hundreds.

On another occasion, Samai, a twelve year old Iban girl, was accidentally blinded when acid, used for curing rubber, splashed in her face. She was brought by longboat to Nangga Gaat, the forward base of 845 Squadron, and flown to Sibu for a medical inspection to see if there was any chance of an eye operation for a corneal graft. Eventually Samai was examined by Dr Leslie, the Kuching eye surgeon and flown to Singapore where she was operated on by Mr Ridley, a London eye surgeon. The result was partially successful.

A happier ending occurred with a fifteen year old boy who was accidentally pierced in the head by a harpoon arrow. To travel by boat to the nearest hospital would have taken many days, so the Royal Navy offered to fly him to Sibu. Because of the harpoon in his head, the boy had to climb sideways into the Wessex. The weather was atrocious, and the helicopter pilots took it in turns to fly through torrential rain in the dark. But thanks to their efforts a successful operation was carried out at Sibu.

The Royal Air Force helicopter squadrons also played their part in winning the hearts and minds of the locals. 225 Squadron, based on Kuching, performed many humanitarian tasks. When a five year old Indonesian boy's thigh was pierced by a sharp bamboo stake, his father, rather than take him to the Indonesian authorities, carried him six miles through the jungle to a Security Force post on the Malaysian border. At once the boy was flown to hospital by helicopter.

The Royal Ulster Rifles carried out a weekly patrolling routine by longboat down the smaller out-of-the-way rivers to visit the people in their longhouses. First-aid was given mostly to the children, but the idea caught on. The troops came to the conclusion that the older locals thought it polite to complain of a headache and be rewarded with a coveted codeine tablet. As one rifleman remarked, 'It is rather similar to a Unionist candidate at a Belfast election trying to win favour through the children.' A Smarties Chocolate Bean made many a sick child happy and recover rapidly.

The Security Forces also helped in other ways. They organized children's parties on land and on board the Commando ships *Albion* and *Bulwark*. The troops contributed ice-cream, orange squash, sweets, and chocolates from their own pockets. The Gurkha pipe bands were always an attraction. At one Christmas party for seventy-eight children at the Methodist

Children's Home, Sibu, Father Christmas arrived by helicopter.

Capt Carson of the Ulster Rifles helped the Ibans in a more material and long-term way. When visiting a local longhouse he was appalled to find that they grew nothing but rice, and that only in a haphazard manner. He also remarked on the way they let their pigs and poultry run wild, and their indiscriminate fishing of the river. Carson set about rectifying their bad habits. He paraded the local inhabitants and with an interpreter harangued them about the error of their ways. He described the advantages of methodical market-gardening, and finally told them to parade the following day with picks and shovels. Earlier he had sent off a request to battalion HQ for vegetable seeds and advice on what to plant and when. The next day half the village turned out and, under Carson's guidance, they set to work with glee. Once the vegetable beds had been organized, Carson turned to the construction of pens for the pigs and coops for the chickens.

The sense of security which the troops brought to the tribes was very important. On one occasion when Brigadier Glennie was spending the night at a longhouse in the Fourth Division, he noticed that the people were worried. He questioned them, and the headman explained, 'We are afraid lest bad people come.' Glennie told them not to worry. There was a wireless set at the airfield, and if any bad men were in the vicinity they had only to let him know on the radio and he would send soldiers. This pleased the locals who wished to hold their children's sports day. Glennie told them to go ahead with the event, and he would present a prize. They hastily poured him out another glass of *tuak* while they went into consultation. Eventually they came back. Yes, they would be delighted if he would present a prize —for the one hundred yards under four feet! It seems that these simple people had overcome the somewhat unfair arrangement in our own civilized world where children's races are run according to age and not size.

Perhaps one of the most humane acts of assistance was rendered by the Royal Ulster Rifles. There was a Dyak village across the border in Kalimantan, and some Indonesian soldiers who were based in its vicinity made periodical visits to 'purchase' food, using strong-arm tactics if nothing was forthcoming. At last the Dyaks held a meeting and decided that they would leave their home, most of their goods and chattels, and cross over into Sarawak. At 2200 on a Saturday night the twenty families, having packed what they could carry, moved off into the jungle. They walked all through the night, and at 1000 the following morning reached a friendly village near B Company of the Ulsters. They were a pathetic sight; tired, their feet bleeding, clothes in tatters, crying babies supported on mothers' hips, and with a lost, bewildered look in their eyes as if they had given up all hope.

The seventy-two refugees were packed into a couple of three-tonners and dispatched to battalion HQ where Major McGonigal of HQ Company took over. He paraded them, segregated them into sexes, and had them medically examined. All were re-clothed, then repacked into the trucks and taken to the local rest house. There the company pitched a marquee for them to live in, dug latrines, collected firewood and gave them some food. By the afternoon there was a remarkable change in their appearance. Once more they looked the happy, carefree, laughing Dyak. They settled down in their new home which became known as Kampong McGonigal.

It was through acts like these that the Security Forces won and kept the admiration of the local tribes throughout Confrontation. And it was one of the major reasons why the Security Forces were able to hold almost one thousand miles of jungle frontier against guerrillas, who were always superior in numbers, without once dropping a bomb or firing a rocket. The Malaysian Government, too, realized that the war could not be won without the people's support. It is to their credit that after the first shaky moments they kept the public informed, so the people knew what the struggle was all about.

NINE

Political and Military Incursions

From the start of Confrontation the Indonesians' plan had been to set up guerrilla pockets in Sarawak which at an appointed time could be called 'liberated areas'. Operation Parrot was a temporary set-back to their aims and the first abortive raids had been countered by the Security Forces. Now the Indonesians began probing eastwards into the Third and Fourth Divisions, and towards Tawau in north-east Sabah. But their main concentration was still on the First and Second Divisions, and this pattern remained more or less constant, with comparatively less activity in Sabah and the other divisions.

The reason was obvious: the border along the First and Second Divisions was less rugged and only fifteen miles from a safe haven in the CCO sectors. Kuching and its airport were only a short distance from the border, and in the beginning it was fairly easy for invaders to infiltrate round the northern tip of Sarawak by sea, although the Royal Navy and the Royal Air Force soon made this considerably more hazardous.

During the early stages of Confrontation, Sukarno had an ally in President Macapagal of the Philippines who laid claim to Sabah. While Sukarno used political gambits for the sole purpose of destroying Malaysia, Macapagal was obviously anxious to reach a peaceful agreement satisfactory to all parties. Through the Philippine President's initiative, a Conference of the Foreign Ministers of the three countries was held in Manila from 7 to 11 June, 1963. This in turn led to a Tripartite Summit Meeting in Manila early in August. On paper it seemed that the meeting had 'resolved various current problems of common concern'.

The Tunku certainly appears to have made every effort to find a peaceful solution. His main step in this direction was to agree to United Nations observers making an impartial enquiry in Sabah and Sarawak as to whether the inhabitants really wished

77

to join Malaysia. He also conceded that the inclusion of Sabah in Malaysia would not prejudice the Philippine 'claim or any right thereunder'. The meeting agreed 'that initial steps should be taken towards the establishment of Maphilindo by holding frequent and regular consultations at all levels to be known as Mushawarah Maphilindo'.

But even during the Summit Meeting Indonesian guerrillas continued to carry out raids across the border. Sukarno intended to use every form of intimidation possible in the few weeks before the arrival of the UN observers, including a major raid in strength towards the end of August.

Koesto, the head of Indonesian Intelligence in Singapore, tried to persuade representatives of anti-Malaysia parties in Singapore and the Federation to attend a mass anti-Malaysia rally in Medan, Sumatra, on 31 August. At his instigation, telegrams of protest were sent to Macapagal during the Manila Conference, saying that Malaysia would not be accepted without a referendum in the Borneo Territories. On the eve of his compulsory departure from Singapore in September, Koesto urged the Peninsula Malay Union 'to unite Malays and local Indonesians in a revolution to overthrow the Tunku's government'.

In the First Division the kampong of Gumbang continued to be a favourite target of the Indonesians as it was only two hundred yards from the border. The post was commanded by Sgt Alastair Mackie of 42 Commando, and his force consisted of a rifle section from L Company and a section of Border Scouts.

In the early hours of 17 August, and again during the nights of the 21st and 22nd, Indonesian raiders attacked the post but were beaten back. Then on the 23rd the rebels prepared to mount a more serious attack with some sixty men. Before they could even reach the post, however, they were ambushed by the Marines and quickly dispersed. This last raid seems to indicate that the Indonesians had decided to use larger groups for their border raids. It also became clear that the volunteers were being led and trained by Indonesian regulars. The Security Forces noticed that leadership had improved, although discipline was still poor and determination was lacking.

That same month, a force from fifty to sixty strong, and strengthened by Tentara Nasional Indonesia (TNI) personnel, crossed the border into the Third Division and moved north towards Song on the Rajang River. This was the first deep incursion with a definite military objective: the capture of Song. It was a tough assignment. The country was very difficult and communications were limited to the rivers.

News of their infiltration near Sungei Bangkit reached the 2/6th Gurkha Rifles, and a patrol from C Company was sent to investigate. Shortly after the patrol's departure, Lt Hugh Wallace, who had only recently arrived in the battalion, joined them by helicopter and took command.

Wallace's patrol moved down-river in search of the enemy. On 16 August contact was made near a kampong, and in the ensuing battle six raiders were killed. During the fight, Wallace led a party round a flank, but was hit in the knee and was unable to move. His orderly remained with him, but he ordered the party to carry on. By now it was growing dark, so Wallace told his orderly to return to the base camp for help. In daylight the journey, through trackless jungle, normally took five hours, so the orderly did well to reach base by the following morning.

When the rescue party arrived Wallace was dead. During the night the Indonesians had found him, and although he had put up a brave fight, a shot through the shoulder had killed him.

A platoon flown in the next day to cut off the raiders' escape route, made immediate contact, and killed three rebels. News began to filter in of the raiders' movements. Thirty-nine of the original group were moving down-river into the eastern half of the Third Division. In the two weeks since they had crossed the border they had only penetrated some ten to fifteen miles, and were tired and hungry.

The Sungei Bangkit incident indicated a strong chance of other deep incursions. Accordingly, Walker flew in the 1/2nd Gurkhas to take over the Third Division, while the two companies of the 2/6th moved into the Fifth Division and Sabah to rejoin their battalion in the 99th Gurkha Brigade group area.

Earlier in June, 846 Squadron had returned to the ship as it was thought they could be relieved by newly arrived RAF helicopter reinforcements. Walker wrote to Cdr Burke, 'I shall be sending a signal to you before you leave, but I shall not regard this as a farewell, because I am certain that Indonesia is up to no good and before long we shall be calling for you once again.'

Prophetic words. The squadron now returned to Kuching to support 42 Commando in the First Division.

Towards the end of August a band of guerrillas came to a longhouse near Song looking for a place to hide. The Pengulu directed them up the Angkuah River, and when they had moved on he reported at once to the 1/2nd Gurkha Rifles Tactical HQ at Song. Two platoons were already in ambush positions up-river, and they started on the trail of the band which, it turned out, had earlier been involved in the action with the 2/6th Gurkhas when Wallace had been killed. The Gurkhas searched relentlessly for forty-eight hours, and on 2 September the leading platoon was moving up the river-bed when it was spotted by the enemy. Fire was exchanged at a range of four hundred yards. One Indonesian was killed and a number of weapons, documents, and packs recovered.

Shortly afterwards a platoon from C Company under Lt Lalitbahadur caught up with a section of the enemy on a steep, jungle-covered slope. His call to surrender was answered by rifle fire which wounded one of his men. At once the Gurkhas attacked. Forcing their way through a mat of undergrowth and thick jungle, they came to grips with the enemy at close quarters and killed five of them.

The following morning, Capt Aitasing of D Company ambushed the bearded leader of the gang and another man, killing both with his Bren gun. On the 4th a further raider was captured with his rifle. The following day an Iban from a near-by longhouse accounted for another with shot-gun and parang. Finally on 18 September, a very tired raider was captured when trying to find his way through the jungle.

Following the Manila Summit Meeting, a nine-man United Nations Team arrived in Kuching on 1 September 1963, together with Philippino and Indonesian observers. They toured the country by helicopter between 2 and 5 September so that they could cover as much ground as possible during their fact-finding mission. In reporting to the Secretary-General, the UNO Team said that it was satisfied that it had reached a wide cross-section of the population of the Borneo territories in all walks of life, and that the expressions of opinion it had heard represented the views of a sizeable majority of the people.

U Thant commented, 'I believe the majority [of the peoples of Sabah and Sarawak] have concluded that they wish to bring their dependent status to an end, and to realize their independence through freely-chosen association, heritage, language, religion, culture, economic relationship, ideals and objectives. Not all these considerations are present in equal weight in all minds, but it is my conclusion that the majority of the peoples of the two territories, having taken them into account, wish to engage with the peoples of the Federation of Malaya and Singapore, in an enlarged Federation of Malaysia through which they can strive together to realize the fulfilment of their destiny. . . .' According to the official Indonesian news agency, the leader of the Indonesian observers said on his return to Djakarta that 'he was convinced of the impartiality of the United Nations Team's work'.

On 16 September 1963, Malaysia was proclaimed. Indonesian reaction was immediate and violent. In Djakarta mobs sacked the British Embassy. The Indonesian Government refused to recognize Malaysia. Diplomatic relations with both Indonesia and the Philippines were broken off by Malaysia. Along the frontier separating Sarawak and Sabah from Kalimantan, Indonesian guerrillas started to intensify their raids.

Thirty miles inside the Third Division was the village of Long Jawai. It was an isolated place on the edge of an ill-mapped and sparsely inhabited area. A Border Scout post had been established, manned by six Gurkhas from the 1/2nd, three regular policemen, and twenty-one Border Scouts. Many of the villagers had originated from the Indonesian side of the border. Besides this, isolated as they were, they had little faith in the ability of the Security Forces to protect them. Kuching was a vague name many days' journey across Sarawak; Kuala Lumpur, for all it meant to them, might as well have been on the moon. Lightly held, and with the inhabitants shaky in their allegiance to Malaysia, the village was an ideal target. While Malaysia was still an unknown quantity a successful attack could have a weakening effect on other longhouses, besides showing up the inefficiency of the Security Forces.

On 26 and 27 September about a hundred and fifty raiders crossed the border undetected, infiltrated into Long Jawai and hid in the longhouses, persuading the inhabitants to keep quiet. On 27 September an officer from the 1/2nd Gurkhas visited the village and spoke to the locals but they gave no hint that they were harbouring armed raiders. During the early hours of 28 September the Indonesians moved stealthily out of the longhouses and approached the Security Force post situated in the school house. At first light a fusillade of MMG and rifle fire raked the building; a bomb from a 60 mm mortar ricochetted off a tree and exploded directly overhead. By ill-luck this killed both the Gurkha and police radio operators and knocked out the radios before a message could be sent. Another Gurkha, a policeman, and a Border Scout were also killed in the first burst of firing. With the exception of one man, the remaining Scouts took to the jungle where they were captured. In the school house, the four Gurkhas, a policeman and the Border Scout, after the initial shock, returned fire. They were not in a viable defensive position, and withdrew further up a hill away from the buildings. There the small band kept the enemy at bay for three hours. But with ammunition running low, and after two more of their number were wounded, they withdrew into the jungle, reaching safety some days later.

News of the attack was brought to the 1/2nd Gurkhas' Battalion HQ on 30 September by a villager and three Border Scouts who had managed to escape from the raiders. It looked as if the Indonesians had dealt a telling blow. But they had not counted on two factors: commanding the Gurkha battalion was Lt-Col Clements, an old jungle hand who had won an MC at Imphal during World War II; and to support the Gurkhas were the helicopters of 845 Royal Naval Squadron.

Clements soon worked out the raiders' escape route to the border. He also decided, after interrogating an escaped Border Scout, that the enemy camp was near the junction of the Jalangai and Balui rivers. He was determined to account for as many of the raiders as possible, and so as not to disturb them he asked the Navy on no account to fly their helicopters over that area during the first week of the hunt.

On 1 October four helicopters roped down Gurkhas into two ambush sites on the Batang Balui, upriver from Long Jawai and on the most likely escape route.

That evening Lt Pasbahadur and 11 Platoon were established

in an ambush position. In the distance they heard the chug of outboard motors, then two longboats came into view packed with armed Indonesians. Executing a perfect ambush, the Gurkhas poured fire into the boats. One sank at once, the other was wrecked on the shore, and all twenty-six men in the boats were killed. A large amount of equipment was removed from the wrecked boat, including a 60 mm mortar, and the two radio sets taken from the dead operators at Long Jawai.

The follow-up platoon found the enemy camp on 12 October. The raiders had gone, leaving behind five of their dead whom they had buried. They also left the mutilated remains of the seven Border Scouts who had been murdered in cold blood. Another enemy corpse was found along the escape route where he had apparently collapsed from exhaustion. The camp had been used by the Indonesians as a hideout from which they would be ferried back to the border in their five powered longboats. Two of the boats were knocked out in the ambush, another was surprised by an Auster near the Balui-Aput junction and later seen to have been abandoned. This left two which got away and presumably did not bother to return for the waiting raiders. After a wait of nearly a week, the remainder must have decided to start the long trek home.

By now the Gurkha follow-up platoon was very weary and was pulled out and replaced by fresh troops who continued the hunt south along the Balui. All this time, Long Jawai was being prepared as a company HQ with reserve troops and rations flown in whenever possible.

On 10 October, the first ambush party up the Aput killed one raider although his companion escaped. It was presumed that these men had come from the abandoned longboat. With the possibility of the retreating Indonesians nearing the border, 845 Squadron landed two Gurkha long-stop ambushes near the boat station at the top end of both the Balui and Aput. These boat stations mark the uppermost navigable reaches of the two rivers; it is the point where traders crossing the border leave their boats, walk over the watershed, and pick up boats at a similar station on the other side.

Three days later it was discovered that the Aput ambush platoon was in the wrong place. It took a further two days to

83

locate them, five miles down the Sungei Kliong, a tributary of the Aput. A power saw was winched down to the platoon from a helicopter to make an LZ. While the saw was being winched down the aircrew suddenly noticed the Gurkhas scatter as a tree which they had been cutting in anticipation of the helicopter's arrival started to fall. The aircrew gave the 'go-up' signal just in time. As the tree crashed into the jungle, the top narrowly missed the wheels of the helicopter. The platoon was in a very awkward position for lifting out, the trees being very high, the valley steep, and the LZ small. Up the river valley, three Indonesians saw the helicopters hovering over the jungle, offering a sitting target, and at once rushed to the area with a Browning MMG. Fortunately, only half-an-hour earlier, a Gurkha platoon had been put down two miles east of the Aput-Kliong junction, and the Indonesians walked into their ambush. One was killed and the other two were wounded but escaped. The machine gun was captured.

By the end of October the remainder of the raiders had escaped, although several must have died in the jungle. News of the Security Forces' amazingly quick reaction, and the results achieved, soon travelled around the longhouses, and the locals took heed. It was a long time before the Indonesians showed themselves in the area again. A postscript to the Long Jawai incident occurred a few months later. As a result of the raid there was a grave shortage of Border Scouts in the Belaga area. Word went around for more, but no one cared to volunteer. John Cross asked the Resident of the Third Division to publicize the vacancies, and if necessary replace the indigenous Kayan and Kenyah stock with Ibans, which would have started a tribal war twenty years earlier! The Resident agreed, and also enlisted the help of Radio Sarawak, the District Officer, the Sarawak Administration Officer and the Pengulus.

When Cross arrived to enroll the recruits he found there were none. He went upstream and spent a night in Long Linau with the Sarawak Administration Officer and met the local dignitaries.

'The inhabitants of the longhouse were morose and disinterested,' said Cross. 'It was as though a pane of glass separated us, and we goggled fish-like at each other. It took me an hour's playing with the children, making them laugh at my funny faces and sleight-of-hand before the thaw started. After four hours I jockeyed the locals into saying that they would serve under their own conditions, which coincided exactly with my own. The recruits reported two weeks later at Belaga.'

serve under their own conditions, which coincided exactly with

TEN
The 'Choppers'

The helicopter was the real battle-winner of Confrontation; without it it would have been impossible for the
Security Forces to control such a vast area against the guerrillas.
Consider the distances and topography involved. A frontage of
1,000 miles, depth 100 miles (excluding Kuching), and long
brigade fronts—companies could be over 100 miles from their
battalion HQ. Over the jungle one hour in a helicopter equalled
at least five days on foot. The Army needed mobility and
flexibility to cope with the guerrillas and helicopters were able
to provide it without risk of ambush. The pilots used contour
flying and acquired considerable skill in setting down the troops
within striking distance of the enemy without being seen or
heard. Once landed, the infantry advanced on foot to close in for
the kill. A clever company commander with a few 'choppers'
could so block the guerrillas at every turn that they would think
an entire army was on their heels. In fact, so often did the
Security Forces hit the enemy as soon as he put his nose across
the border, that they were even credited with having special
radar! A battalion with six Wessex was worth more to a
Director of Operations than a brigade without helicopters. But
they were always at a premium. The total number in Borneo was
never more than 100, which is about 2,700 less than the troop-
carrying helicopters available in South Vietnam. Had six helicopters been available per battalion, Confrontation might well
have finished a year earlier.

The most important tactical innovation involving the use of
helicopters was the concept of forward deployment and decentralization, that is to say, keeping the machines with the
forward troops instead of flying them in and out from a central-
ized base as required. It offered several advantages: there were
no dead flying hours; pilots became personally familiar with the

country and able to approach unheard and unseen; pilots completely identified themselves with day-to-day operations as well as with ground commanders at every level; and forward deployment ensured an instantaneous response to every alarm and emergency. There is no doubt that decentralization resulted in an immediacy and flexibility which could never otherwise have been achieved.

Perhaps this is not surprising. The helicopter, after all, is just as much a weapon as the tank or self-propelled gun. It became more than mere transport; it was absolutely vital to every commander's plan at all levels. Most aircraft fight in the upper air in accordance with the environment of the air battle; helicopters fight in the lower air in accordance with the environment of the land battle. Accordingly, it was imperative that ground commanders be permitted to influence the helicopter's allocation and control, and to integrate its operations intimately into ground operations. Once an operation was launched, command had to be vested in one person, and that person could only be the commander in whose environment the battle was being fought— namely the infantry commander.

Life was not easy for the 'chopper' pilot or for the ground crew, and it was to the great merit of the Royal Navy and the Royal Air Force that so much success was achieved. A good picture of the situation can be formed from the activities of 845 Royal Naval Squadron commanded by Lt-Cdr G. J. Sherman, inevitably nick-named 'Tank', who, indeed, pioneered the whole concept of the forward deployment and decentralization of helicopters. The squadron was equipped with Westland Wessex Mark 1 helicopters (Napier Gazelle gas-turbine engines) which, until the arrival some time later of the Mark II, were the most efficient in Borneo from the point of view of payload and serviceability.

Weather was the greatest drawback to operations. The valleys were invariably full of cloud, often down to ground level until mid-forenoon. In the late afternoon thunderstorms started to build up and with the approach of the north-east monsoon the weather deteriorated to a point where flying periods were limited sometimes to between 1130 and 1500. The incredibly rugged terrain consisted mainly of ridges two to three thousand feet high, with an occasional mountain range rising from four to six thousand feet and almost invariably partly, if not wholly, obscured by cloud. One ridge in particular, eight miles long and rising to four thousand feet at the western end, was a serious obstacle. On several occasions pilots, low on fuel after a long sortie, nearly crashed on this ridge. To counter this, Gurkha engineers constructed an emergency LZ on a two thousand five hundred foot plateau to the south of the range.

Another feature of operations was the distances involved. Most platoons were put in at a range of sixty to eighty miles, and to do this in one lift meant overweight running take-offs from the airstrip. The standard payload was eight troops plus kit (200 lb each) plus 1,800 lb fuel. Airfield temperature was usually thirty to thirty-four degrees Centigrade. Wind never exceeded five knots.

Nine times out of ten the LZs were shingle banks by rivers. Usually these were quite suitable, but sometimes disappeared when the rivers rose after rain. Although the trees were high, and the valleys often steep, a river usually provided a good entry and exit lane.

The LZs cut out of the jungle by the Gurkhas invariably started as a vertical *tube* through the trees, sometimes one hundred and forty to one hundred and fifty feet long, and wide enough to fit one Wessex all the way down with perhaps five feet to spare all round! According to Lt Steil, RN, 'The Gurkhas did very well considering the only equipment they had were kukris and machettes, but eventually they got the message that an approach and exit lane was needed!'

Maps were almost useless. The main rivers were marked, but sometimes quite inaccurately. Very few of the myriad of small rivers were shown; and the mountain ranges were completely inaccurate except for spot heights. In fact ninety per cent of the maps was white paper. Even Belaga airstrip was two miles out of position and on the wrong side of the river. One newly-arrived company commander remarked: 'This isn't a map, it's a Naval Chart!' All of this made it extremely difficult for the pilots to find patrols already in the jungle, but they did marvellous work in tracking them down.

The best technique evolved in bad conditions, particularly where a LZ had to be cut quickly to rescue a serious casualty case, was to establish a hover above the site while a second helicopter positioned above. The pilot of the first aircraft then lowered gently into the clearing, like descending in a lift, being voice-marshalled by the pilot in the other aircraft. Sometimes because of obstruction in the clearing the aircraft had to make a low hover—that is, remain a few feet above the ground while troops deplaned or emplaned. It was not always possible to get so close to the ground. On one occasion a party of SAS rushed out with a fifteen foot home-made ladder, propped it alongside the helicopter and climbed up.

845 Squadron's main base was at Sibu, usually with five Wessex and one Auster ashore. Relations between the Navy, Army, Police and local civilians could not have been better. The ratings, on their own initiative, painted the badge of the 1/2nd Gurkha Rifles on every helicopter. At the Royal Naval Air Station, Sibu, known as HMS *Hornbill*, the crossed kukris of 17th Gurkha Division were engraved on the white ensign. The squadron's forward base was first situated at Belaga, but this threw a great strain on the RAF's airdrop resources. The alternative was to move to another spot which could be supplied by longboat, and thus release the RAF who, in turn, could take over the supply drop to Long Jawai.

A reconnaissance suggested that Nangga Gaat would make a suitable forward base. It was situated at an important river junction, strategically placed as far forward as possible to cover the border and still maintain the precious river line. It was also the home of the Temonggong Jugah, Paramount Chief of the Ibans. At first sight, however, there seemed little enough at Nangga Gaat to commend it as a helicopter base. The village was located on a small, grassy promontory and surrounded by primary jungle. There was no room to land—the advance party had to use the river bed. But the squadron party set to work with the help of local labour to cut down trees, and prepare six landing points on the lower level suitable for a light maintenance and refuelling point. They also cleared two hilltop landing points with a suitable 'drive-away' to permit maximum weight take-offs. In the end it proved a highly satisfactory forward base. Between Sibu and Nangga Gaat the whole of the Third Division was now within the one hundred mile radius of the Wessex.

Accommodation at Nangga Gaat was practically non-existent. At first a partly-filled timber shed was used as the Operations

Room and Air Maintenance Office. A Chinese trader's quarters were partly taken over as junior rates accommodation and dining-room and galley for all. Wood-fired and boiling 'ovens' were constructed from forty-four-gallon drums embedded in cement. The officers slept under the Temonggong's bungalow, senior ratings slept in a tent. An early discovery was a 240-volt generator, owned by the Temonggong. But it was in very bad condition and had not worked for a long time. With the assistance of the PWD at Sibu, the generator was coaxed into life and there was electricity for all.

When it became apparent that Nangga Gaat was to be a permanent base, the squadron set to work to make it habitable. Seven huts were built on stilts with split bamboo floors and *atap* roofs. There were goats in a near-by compound and numerous pet dogs; the duckboard path was often impeded by a recumbent water buffalo.

The officers lived in two adjacent huts accommodating five each. Next door was the Chief Petty Officers' and Petty Officers' Mess. Across the pathway a long building housed the Ratings' Mess in the larger room and a communal dining-hall in the smaller. There was a galley and a small wire-enclosed pantry. The wood-fired 'ovens' were replaced by a petrol cooker set in a hole in the ground and covered with an *atap* roof. Water was pumped from the river and purified by filtering through a complicated system of old fuel drums. Hot and cold water was available on a time basis. 'If you took a shower in the early dogs when the sun had been on the tank all day you got hot water,' said Sherman. 'Until the late dogs the water was pleasantly warm; but in the early morning it was either refreshing or *bloody* cold!'

The centre of Camp 845's pride and joy was *The Anchor Inn*, whose hospitality became renowned not only in South-east Asia, but also in England through the cartoons of 'Jak' in the *Evening Standard*. *The Anchor Inn* was an *atap* hut, containing a central bar and two rooms—one for junior ratings, the other for officers and senior rates. Segregation, however, was strictly enforced only for the first five minutes after opening time. The men could either recline in comfortable home-made arm-chairs or, after a few drinks, move on to the nightly film show. The chiefs and petty officers usually stayed in the *Anchor*—'To see that it didn't burn down!' To maintain the prestige of the white man in the East, everyone dressed for dinner: flip-flops, sarongs, and native beads!

Life was not all relaxation. It centred around the helicopters seven days a week; maintaining the machines in operational order, and flying them at a moment's notice, was a tough assignment. Work started at daybreak and continued usually up to 1800 hours or even later if necessary. When the helicopters returned from the last mission of the day they had to be prepared for the next day's flight before the ground crews knocked off. Once work finished, however, they made the best of their situation. Midnight was the approximate closing time. Then everyone headed for bed, collecting a small pile of stones on the way to throw at the cocks which usually started crowing at dawn.

During their stay at Nangga Gaat, the personnel of 845 Squadron became well known among the longhouses and kampongs in the area, often forming an amazing bond of friendship. When, early in 1965, the squadron had its first accident, the local people of Nangga Gaat, on their own initiative, went into mourning for a month because of their love for the dead pilot and his companions. During that period no gongs were beaten and no parties were held.

From December, 1962, the time it first went ashore at Brunei, to early 1965 the squadron completed ten thousand hours' operational flying; carried over fifty thousand passengers and six million pounds of stores, and flew over five hundred casualties—forty of them at night in appalling weather. The squadron had been detached from both *Albion* and *Bulwark* to seven different bases, and over one period had operated from four different locations at one time. It was not until the end of its tour, that the squadron suffered any accidents. Then tragically in the months of February, March, and April 1965 five aircraft crashed, killing three pilots, two aircrewmen and eleven soldiers. The average of 88 per cent serviceability achieved through the two years was only made possible by the highest standards of maintenance. In 1964, 845 Squadron was awarded the coveted Boyd Trophy, an annual award given for the finest contribution to Naval Aviation. This was a double honour for the Navy's helicopters, since the same award had been made to Commander Burke's 846 Squadron the previous year.

ELEVEN
Nemesis in Tawau

After Malaysia Day it was possible to supplement the Security Forces with Malaysian Regiments. The 3rd Battalion Royal Malay Regiment was sent to Tawau. The 5th Battalion was posted to the First Division to take over responsibility for the whole of the Serian and Sadong Districts from 40 Commando. B Squadron of the Federal Recce Regiment, commanded by Major Baljit Singh, took over a border post, relieving a Commando troop which was placed in their support. In like manner every effort was made to integrate British and Federation forces.

During the next few months there were no major incursions, and little border activity apart from the occasional minor assault on an outpost. There were, however, two blatant incursions by the Indonesian Air Force. On 13 November a B-25 and two Mustang fighters buzzed several positions along the First Division border. The second incident occurred when a TU-16 Badger circled Kuching at a height of 4,000 feet and then flew off in a south-westerly direction.

The Indonesians also fired on several Security Force aircraft near the border. On 16 December an Auster on a training flight over the Lundu District was attacked by ground fire. Sgt Thakeray, the pilot, was hit in the arm. His passenger, an RAF padre, was hit in the chest. Thackeray, in spite of his wound, managed to fly for about seven minutes to the nearest patrol base. After two attempts to land on a helicopter LZ, using his knees to operate the joystick, his third effort was successful. Unfortunately, the padre died soon after the landing.

The internal threat was ever-present, and continual checks by Security Forces and police were necessary as the CCO were still training where possible. The coastline was a back door into Sarawak for groups sent to train and rouse the CCO cells into

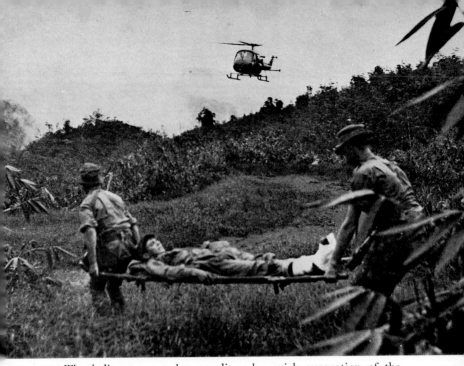

8. The helicopter saved many lives by quick evacuation of the wounded.

9. The forward bases were built almost on the style of First World War fortifications, with communication trenches and deep dug-outs.

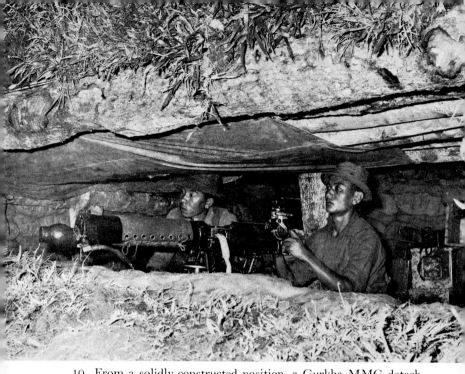

10. From a solidly-constructed position, a Gurkha MMG detachment guards a border post.

11. Infantry support was given on many occasions by the armoured regiments. Here Saladin armoured cars of 4 RTR fire on jungle trails in the distant hills.

activity. One party of six Indonesians and Chinese who had infiltrated by sea, were captured by the Special Branch in Simmangang. They had been in the area for some time, but became discouraged because of the lack of support and by the tight security control over movement.

In December, Brigadier Barton handed over command of West Brigade to Brigadier Patterson of 99 Gurkha Brigade.

Although Indonesian guerrilla activity was confined mainly to West Sarawak in 1963 the situation around Tawau, in the Tawau Residency of Sabah, had to be watched closely. In October it was reported that the Indonesians were definitely planning operations in that area. No. 2 Special Boat Section Royal Marines, commanded by Capt D. W. Mitchell, moved at thirty-six hours' notice from Singapore to Tawau. Mitchell's task was to patrol the river complex to the north-west of Sebatik Island and prevent any attempts at infiltration from the Indonesian island of Nanukan. He stayed in the area until 20 December, by which time he had trained an assault boat team of ten coxswains from the 3rd Royal Malay Regiment to carry out small boat patrols in the area. During this period a good deal of small boat traffic was stopped. No fighting occurred, apart from one occasion when an Indonesian LMG opened fire at a range of two thousand yards, but no one was hit.

For some time, Sukarno's eye had been on Tawau. His aim was to wreck the economy and so ruin Malaysia. Tawau was the main town in the Tawau Residency of Sabah, one of the most prosperous areas of East Malaysia. There was a vast hinterland of estates: logging concerns, tea estates, rubber plantations, cocoa, oil palm, and hemp. The Indonesian border was very close. Across the Cowie Harbour lay Sebatik Island, the northern half Malaysian, the southern Indonesian. At the northern tip was the important logging station at Wallace Bay, only some four miles from the border. At that time a strong commando raid could probably have burnt out the station.

The area around Tawau was a mass of mangrove swamps and tidal rivers which emptied into Cowie Harbour at the eastern end of which lay Tawau. Some forty miles north-west of Tawau, was the Bombay Burma logging centre at Kalabakan, the main centre of population in the western sector of the Residency. The

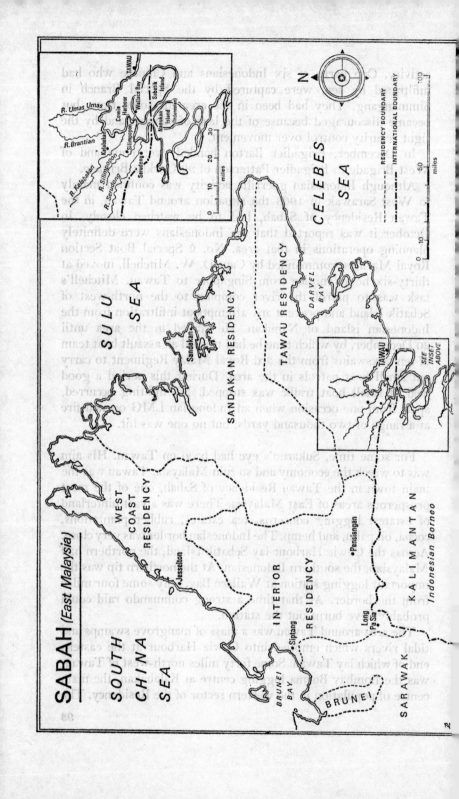

total population in 1963 was about 15,000, some three-fifths of whom were Indonesians.

To the north of Kalabakan, there were logging camps at Wellawatta, Mawan, 12th and 16th Milestones, and at Brantian which had a straggling village downstream from the logging camp. All the camps were connected by a network of gravel roads with small and often overgrown tracks leading from the roads in use. None of these roads was marked on any maps held by the Security Forces.

The majority of the area was primary jungle, the rest either mangrove swamp or secondary jungle where logging had already taken place. This secondary jungle produced some of the most difficult going the Security Forces had ever met for debris from tree felling had to be contended with in addition to the normal heavy undergrowth. The hills were steep, rising at an average to fifteen hundred feet and with a thick covering of jungle. The rivers were tidal for some ten miles upstream, producing drinking water problems, and on the ebb resulted in fast flowing streams. The area was sparsely populated, apart from the estates. On the Serudong River, near the border south of Kalabakan, there were two centres of population: one at Serudong Laut, with about a hundred villagers made up of Tidongs and Muruts; the other at Serudong Ulu, a scattered village of some two hundred Muruts.

On the Umas Umas River, between Kalabakan and Tawau, a new logging camp had been established about seven miles from the mouth of the river, with a mixed population of some two hundred. A dry-weather track had been cut to join up with the roads in the estate complex. These estates were run by the Commonwealth Development Corporation, and covered some 25,000 acres, employing 7,000 Indonesian workers, and producing rubber, hemp, cocoa and oil palm. Most of the area was badly overgrown and offered innumerable hiding places. All these populated areas were potential sources of food for guerrilla bands.

Towards the end of the year, the Security Forces in the area consisted of the 3rd Royal Malay Regiment, a company of the 1st KOYLI, and a rifle group and four scout cars from the 2nd Federation Recce Regiment. A frigate was on permanent station at Tawau for anti-piracy work. The whole of this area was the responsibility of East Brigade, commanded by Brigadier Glennie, who was also in command of Central Brigade.

Sabah, with a labour force of some 25,000 Indonesians, appeared to have a ready-made reservoir for espionage recruits. In 1962, an Indonesian Consulate had been opened in Jesselton, capital of the then British Colony. Later evidence showed that the staff was particularly large for the size of the territory and that many were acting as intelligence agents. The agents centred particular attention on the Indonesian Associations in Labuan, Sandakan, Tawau and Jesselton until they were gradually converted from social and cultural organizations into potential instruments of subversion.

In May, 1963, recruitment began for trainees to go to Djakarta for military training. Plans were discussed to import arms from Kalimantan to Sabah and for border raids. Acts of sabotage were planned to take place in Sandakan and other towns to give the impression that the people opposed the formation of Malaysia. It was also suggested that small groups of guerrillas should cross into Sabah to operate all over the country in close co-operation with members of the Indonesian community. Details of these plans were disclosed by Mohamed Kassim, President of the Indonesian Association in Sandakan, when he was arrested in July, 1963.

The Consulate's subversive activities were not confined to the Indonesian community. Contact was also made with the local Chinese Associations and indigenous groups who were told that an uprising on the lines of the Brunei Revolt was imminent. In July, 1963, the most active Indonesian agents, Major Moenardjo and Mr Bambang Sumali, were expelled; and in September, when Malaysia came into being, the Consulate was closed.

The main source for agents then became the Indonesian immigrants. These labourers had come over to find more work and better conditions and most of them wished to live a quiet life. They were not a Fifth Column as some people suspected, but agents had been infiltrated among them, and although many of these were uncovered by brilliant Special Branch work, the number was growing alarmingly.

By October, 1963, the Indonesians had opened several

volunteer training camps in East Kalimantan across the border from Sabah. To secure recruits, a general publicity campaign was launched in East Kalimantan. Accompanied by incitement against Malaysia through all propaganda media, appeals for volunteers were posted in government offices, flashed on cinema screens, and displayed in villages in an area where unemployment was high.

Former Indonesian immigrants from the Tawau labour force were promised land in Sabah when the territory was eventually taken over. The campaign produced few real volunteers. The more usual method of recruiting, therefore, became impressment. Indonesian barter traders were arrested as smugglers and offered service as an alternative to imprisonment. Men who had served prison sentences, and were known to have a knowledge of Sabah, were rounded up and persuaded to volunteer. Ex-members of the Tawau labour force were given the choice of either joining up or being sent to jail. The 'volunteers' were formed into units known as *Pramukas*. The training and organization was placed in the hands of the TNI and the Korps Komando Operasi [Marines] (KKO).

In mid-December, 1963, the Indonesians decided to send a commando force to capture Kalabakan, then move on to Tawau and Sandakan. This decision was based more on political expediency than on military preparedness. The amount of training given to the *Pramukas* involved was in no case more than eight weeks. Some had received only five days' military instruction and had not fired any live ammunition; some had as little as two days' training and had not even practised loading and unloading. Regardless of this unpreparedness, a force was assembled for the raid. It consisted of one hundred and twenty-eight men, mostly volunteers, but with a stiffening of thirty-five Indonesian regulars, and was divided into four detachments:

N 1. Commanded by Benny, a sergeant in the KKO, thirty-six troops, including eight KKO.

N 2. Commanded by Wayang, thirty-six strong with fifteen KKO.

W 1. Commanded by Lasani, thirty-four strong.

W 2. Commanded by Buronto, a KKO sergeant, and twenty-two strong.

Moving out of their camp in Kalimantan, they crossed the

border to reach Serudong on 21 December. They raided a shop, then moved on to Silimpopon. On 26 December they managed to shoot a wild boar for food. During the night of 28 December they rested at a timber camp near Kalabakan.

In Kalabakan there was a Police Field Force post, wired-in and sandbagged, and manned by fifteen policemen. It was sited overlooking the river. Four hundred yards away was a temporary military post, consisting of two huts with trenches alongside one of them, but no wire. The post was held by a platoon and two sections of 3 RMR under their C Company Commander.

After night fall on 29 December, Benny led his detachment into the attack from two axes. The first group moved along the high ground to the north and worked down the ridge where the RMR position was sited. A section was left at the top of the ridge and moved along the west shoulder, rifling houses for loot and food. The second group moved off the ridge and went north of the police post.

At 2055 the first group hurled grenades into the two huts occupied by the Malay regiment, following this with heavy small arms fire, which killed eight of the soldiers, including the company commander, and wounded nineteen.

The second group did not attack until ten minutes later, and this lack of co-ordination gave the police corporal a chance to rush nineteen police and Home Guard into the compound before the fight developed. The Indonesians threw grenades over the wire, and attempted to scale the wire-fence but the police kept them out, killing one and wounding four. The fight lasted for about two hours, before the guerrillas withdrew from the town, taking with them large quantities of rice. On their way north they met a civilian Landrover bringing labourers from a logging camp. Because the labourers failed to de-bus quickly enough, one was killed and another wounded.

Benny commandeered three of the civilians to guide his party in the direction of Brantian about ten miles north-east of Kalabakan. Three of his own wounded were instructed to make their own way back to Kalimantan, but first he made them change into civilian clothes. Although the groups' morale was high, discipline was slacking off.

Kalabakan, as an important logging centre, had been a good

target for a terrorist attack, but once this had been delivered the element of surprise was lost. If the raiders had moved through the jungle to Tawau direct, the results might have been more effective. But having made the attack they should have moved from the area as quickly as possible. Yet, seven days later, Benny's group and Wayang's group were still less than eight miles north of Kalabakan. They and the other groups were soon to pay the price of their carelessness. They were soon to encounter Lt-Col Burnett of the 1/10th Gurkha Rifles, the Tawau Assault Group and the mangrove swamp death-trap.

At 1230 on 2 January, 1964, the 1/10th Gurkha Rifles received its marching orders, and by four o'clock had started the long move to Tawau. Burnett was at Kalabakan by 1120 the next day. Within twenty-three hours of the first notice that his battalion would be required to deal with the raiders, he had been briefed and had completed an air reconnaissance of the area.

Shortly after Burnett's arrival in Kalabakan, a KOYLI patrol returned to report that they had found a recently-evacuated camp for twenty to thirty men. The group had apparently moved off in a northerly direction. Other reports indicated that a gang had eaten a large quantity of chickens upstream from Kalabakan, and there were rumours of more Indonesians immediately south of the logging town.

Burnett decided that Brantian must be the next place on the raiders' 'shopping list', and so he sent a Gurkha platoon to change over with a Malay platoon stationed there; a KOYLI platoon also remained there to guard the village shop. By last light on 4 January, B and C Companies of the 1/10th had arrived in Kalabakan. Meanwhile all possible 'food points' north of the town had to be denied to the raiders. Wellawatta was cleared of all its civilians and their goods; while from Mawang and the villages at 12th and 16th Milestones the population and all Bombay Burma mechanical equipment was brought in under escort. In Kalabakan, positions were properly dug and wired.

Burnett decided that the first killing ground would be in the area bounded by the triangle: Kalabakan–Mawang–Brantian. A cordon of ambushes was formed on the road from Wellawatta

99

to Mawang, and then eastwards along the road to Brantian; the ambushes were in position by 1600 on 5 January.

Within this triangle were groups N 1 and N 2. W 1 had crossed downstream and headed for Umas Umas; W 2 had decided to escape through the mangrove swamps. In the triangle, the Gurkhas pressed on relentlessly from 7 to 17 January, driving the raiders into the cordon of ambushes and destroying their will to fight. By 17 January fifteen IBTs had been killed and six captured. Except for W 1, the groups started to move back to Indonesia, the survivors of N 1 and N 2 heading west for the Serudong River. Burnett at once moved a company into the area of the Silimpopon River, while another covered the Serudong River. Sufficient troops were left to watch the Brantian, Mawang, and 12th Milestone village area. Both Wellawatta and the 16th Milestone village were razed to the ground to deprive the raiders of any shelter or food.

Of the W 1 detachment, some sixteen managed to reach the estate complex. Four of these were accounted for, six still remained to be found by the end of February and six more were thought to have moved into the Semporna area. W 2, attempting to escape through the mangrove swamps, were severely dealt with by the Tawau Assault Group (TAG) which had been formed by Glennie after the Kalabakan raid. TAG was made up of Malay Patrol craft, and vessels of all types loaned by residents, the government and others in Tawau. The craft were manned by naval personnel with an assault element supplied by the 1/10th Gurkhas. Throughout January the small boats patrolled the mangrove swamp. Part of the 'squadron' was an enormous raft called *Monitor* which mounted a 3-inch mortar. In the channel, the frigate fired star shells and aircraft dropped flares to watch for any attempted escape or infiltration by Indonesian craft to rescue their men.

By the end of February ninety-six of the one hundred and twenty-eight Indonesian raiders had been killed or captured. Twelve still remained at large, although probably with little chance of survival, and twenty had managed to recross the border to safety. At least twenty-one of the thirty-five Indonesian Marines with the four detachments were accounted for; and among those killed were the leaders of W 1 and N 2— Lasani and Wayang. The raid had shown the dangers of com-

100

mando infiltration in the area, but had also shown that the Security Forces could handle an emergency with great speed.

The use of regular Indonesian soldiers was firmly established by the Kalabakan raid. The Indonesian answer to the charge was that certain patriots and sympathizers with the oppressed people of Sabah and Sarawak had shed their military commitments and joined the volunteers. The statements of Marines captured on the raid destroyed this fiction.

The KKO prisoners also revealed that they had been told to expect help and food from local people who were 'discontented' with Malaysia. But they received none, which contravened one of the principles of guerrilla warfare: the infiltrating guerrillas should 'swim in the waters of the friendly inhabitants'.

At the time of the raid Azahari suddenly made an appearance in Pontianak, West Kalimantan, with Dr Subandrio, the Indonesian Foreign Minister. Since his flight from Manila to Djakarta in January, 1963, little had been heard from the leader of the ill-fated Brunei Revolt. During a press conference at Pontianak, Azahari strongly denied that the Indonesian National Army and the CCO were engaged in the border war. It seems obvious, nevertheless, that he was produced with the express purpose of lending cover to the Kalabakan raid which was the prelude and the accompaniment to the diplomatic negotiations conducted by Subandrio at the beginning of 1964.

TWELVE
End of Stage One

Besides their attempts to infiltrate into the Tawau Residency, the Indonesians also probed the Interior Residency and the Fifth Division.

At Bakelalan, in the Fifth Division, a platoon of the 1st Royal Leicestershire Regiment, under 2/Lt Alan Thompson, received several reports during December that the rebels had moved an MMG into the border area. Towards the end of the month Thompson found the MMG site and, after a careful detour, he and his lance-corporal surprised four Indonesians in a *basha* near by, killed them all and destroyed the MMG.

Early on 23 January a Border Scout patrol reported an enemy camp for at least two hundred men near Long Miau in the Interior Residency of Sabah. It had apparently been occupied forty-eight hours previously and signs indicated that the Indonesians had departed towards the north. At once 2/Lt Michael Peele and ten men from 6 Platoon of the 1st Royal Leicesters were flown into Long Pa Sia. At this border post, three thousand feet up in the mountains, they were joined by eight men from 9 Platoon and two Border Scouts. Peele was ordered to try and pick up the enemy's tracks from the area of the camp, follow up with all speed and attack.

The patrol reached the Indonesian's camp at 0900 on the 24th. Signs on various trees indicated that the enemy had moved north, but there were also fresh tracks leading east. Peele decided to follow the east-bound tracks at full speed and to make for faster travel ordered his men to dump their packs. About one and a half hours later they found another camp which had held about eighty men, and the tracks leading out of it were only a day old. Relentlessly Peele led his men along the narrow, winding track through the tangle of jungle. Suddenly three shots rang out somewhere ahead but seemingly were not directed at

102

the patrol. The Border Scouts decided, however, that they would come no further. The Leicesters pressed on, even more alert now, until they heard sounds of movement. About seventy-five yards through the trees two bashas came into view, with more apparently beyond along the side of a stream. There was no way of knowing exactly how many enemy were in the camp, although the number could not be much less than eighty.

The time was now 1300, and as his party had not been seen Peele decided to try and move a strong cut-off group round the rear of the camp before making an assault. He told Cpl Walton to take an LMG and seven men and work his way round to the right of the camp and find a suitable cut-off position within the next hour when the attack would go in. As soon as Walton had moved off, the eleven strong assault group approached the camp carefully. Peele had appreciated that he would have to attack on a narrow front as there were no suitable positions on either flank. A twenty-minute crawl brought them to within forty yards of the camp. But at that moment an unarmed raider who had been answering a call of nature came out of the jungle and stumbled onto the assault group.

Realizing that surprise had now been lost, Peele shot him and shouted to his group to charge straight through the camp firing from the hip. As they broke into the open a Browning automatic chattered out from the area of the first basha and rifle bullets whined across the clearing. Disregarding these, Peele ran on, shouting to one group to get to the flank and give covering fire. The Browning gunner was in position behind a tree but was killed by a bullet from Pte Tinsley's SL Rifle which passed through the eighteen-inch diameter trunk. The jungle echoed with the blast of fire as the assault group passed right through to the other end of the camp, killing four more of the enemy including a section leader. Two of the Indonesians put in a courageous counter-attack, but when one was killed the other fled to safety. The assault group then returned through the camp looking for further enemy troops but found none. There were no tracks even, for most of the enemy had fled into the jungle in small groups when the attack started. The camp scene was one of considerable confusion because the Indonesians had been caught preparing their midday meal. Thirty-seven complete mess kits and another eleven half mess kits were found.

Weapons, ammunition, and equipment lay everywhere—including thirty-five sarongs and a black bus-conductor-type hat. From the evidence the enemy's strength was put at between fifty and sixty.

Peele now decided to return to Long Pa Sia. He had been out of communication since the previous night and there was no suitable LZ near by. The next day he returned to the camp with explosives and blew out an LZ so that the captured arms and ammunition, which weighed over half a ton, could be lifted out.

Besides their attempted incursions across the land frontier the Indonesians continued with their policy to foment internal strife. One way of doing this was by smuggling in arms by sea. Early in January 1964 an Indonesian sergeant set out in a kotak with ten Indonesians and thirteen Sarawak Malaysians who had previously crossed the border into Kalimantan for training. They moved on to the mouth of the Rajang in the Third Division; their aim was to arm and train militant groups in two local Communist organizations: BCP (Borneo Communist Party) and BPS (Barisan Pemuda Sarawak).

News of their arrival reached the Special Branch. But A Company of the 1/7th Gurkhas, who were responsible for the area, had departed some miles up the Rajang on an operation. At once the Special Branch Officer at Sarikei set off to catch up with the Gurkhas and he eventually contacted their company commander, Major O'Leary, who returned immediately to his base at Sarikei.

By this time the raiders had been warned by local Communists, and the Indonesian sergeant decided to split up his party. One section went into temporary hiding on a swampy island in an off-shoot of the Rajang, while the other two moved upstream. The section on the island was discovered by the Special Branch, and O'Leary decided to attack. His plan was for Company HQ in the launch *The Jolly Bachelor* to give covering fire two hundred yards off the north face of the island while 2 and 3 Platoons assaulted the west face.

At 1700 on 7 January both platoons were landed on the island and realized at once that it would be a tough operation. The island was covered with extremely close mangrove which limited visibility. Suddenly one of the raiders opened fire,

104

wounding a Gurkha but pinpointing his own position. A fierce close-quarter fight developed amidst the knotted mangrove and the black, foul-smelling swamp mud. A Gurkha light-machine-gun group came under heavy fire from four automatic weapons. Rifleman Sherbahadur Limbu exposed himself at short range to the full weight of hostile fire in order to bring his Bren gun into action.

The raiders held the advantage as the mangrove cover made them almost invisible to the naked eye. Cpl Shamsherbahadur Limbu, one of the platoon commanders, was badly wounded. He lay in the slush only thirty yards from the enemy. At once the Bren gunner, Sherbahadur, went to his corporal's assistance, but a bullet hit him in the chest, bowling him over into the mud where he lay for two hours, the wound in his chest causing him great pain, his shirt soaked in blood, but still with enough spirit to shout encouragement to his men and his wounded corporal.

In *The Jolly Bachelor* O'Leary had first directed covering fire in an attempt to keep the raiders' heads down, but when he saw that the platoons were held up, he came ashore. Leading one of the platoons to within a few yards of the still invisible enemy he inspired the men with his cool courage, and personally captured a determined terrorist who had defended himself with automatic fire and hand grenades. O'Leary then moved across to Shamsherbahadur's platoon and gave orders for a change in the direction of attack. Obediently, some of the Gurkhas worked their way round to the rear of the enemy and attacked with grenades. As the explosions died down O'Leary went forward boldly, calling on the enemy to surrender.

Three of the raiders were killed during the fight, two wounded and one captured. The seventh man was not found. All three of the Gurkha wounded eventually made good recoveries thanks to their prompt evacuation. One LMG, one Sten and two Armalite rifles were also captured.

Eight days later the remainder of the invaders were moving upriver in the hold of a fishing-boat. A very alert marine inspector recognized it as one which had been reported as stolen. He quickly picked up a boarding party of the Police Field Force and Gurkhas of A Company from their base camp and pursued the enemy. When challenged the fishing-boat failed to stop and had to be rammed. The sixteen raiders on board surrendered without a fight. This successful conclusion to the operation was a good example of the close co-operation between the Security Forces and the Police.

On 16 January, 1964, the Secretary-General of the United Nations appealed to the President of Indonesia and the Prime Minister of Malaysia to bring hostilities to an end. Sukarno agreed to call a truce to allow the Foreign Ministers of both countries to meet for talks in Bangkok. The effective date for the Ceasefire was 25 January. This uneasy truce ended the first year of operations in Borneo. 'A year', wrote General Walker at the time, 'which began with the end of a revolution and ended with the beginning of an undeclared war. No one knows where this exercise in brinkmanship will end. We are sure only of one thing: we have set our faces to the enemy, and until more reasonable counsels prevail, we shall not look back.'

THIRTEEN
Track 6, Blunt, and Sabre Tooth

The uneasy truce ended with the failure of the peace talks in Bangkok, and command of Confrontation operations passed completely to the Indonesian Regular Army. The general pattern of tactics remained the same, with large groups attempting deep penetration to set up guerrilla posts, and shallower incursions to terrorize the locals; but there were now a greater number of regulars in the volunteer units, and TNI battalions also began to take a more active part. This soon became obvious when on several occasions the enemy counter-attacked fiercely and skilfully for the first time since Confrontation began.

The Kling Kang Range, rising to two thousand feet in places, splits the Indonesian border with Sarawak in the Second Division. In the evening of 6 March 1964 some Ibans from a longhouse near the border saw a spiral of grey smoke rising above the jungle on one of the hills in the range. As there were no natives in that area, they reported the incident to the Security Forces.

When Major Ian Mayman, commanding A Company of the 2/10th Gurkha Rifles, received the information he thought at first that it might be a party of CCO who only the previous month had gone into Kalimantan for training. Alternatively, it could be a small reconnaissance party attempting to make contact with local sympathizers prior to a larger incursion by Indonesian forces.

Two tracks, known as 6 and 6A, led from the hill where the smoke had been seen. Any party probing deeper into Sarawak would have to use one of these tracks which were four hundred yards apart and separated by a sheer escarpment. Accordingly, 2 Platoon under Lt (QGO) Karamdhoj Sunwar, was ordered to set ambushes on both tracks near the foot of the hill. If nothing

happened by first light Karamdhoj was to move the ambushes
further up the hill—two sections and HQ up Track 6, the remaining section up Track 6A.

At 0830 Mayman moved to the bottom of Track 6 with his
HQ and called up Karamdhoj on the wireless. The Gurkha
lieutenant reported, 'There are sounds of music from a radio and
of messages being passed on a wireless set coming from the top
of the hill, Sahib.'

'In that case,' said Mayman, 'have a look at the enemy position. If you think you can handle it yourself, attack. If not,
remain in observation and let me know.'

Karamdhoj sent out reconnaissance patrols at once. Two
hours later they reported that a large enemy force was established on the top of a formidable rocky outcrop. By this time the
raiders had detected the presence of the platoon and had stood
to in readiness for an attack.

Meanwhile, Mayman had called forward 1 Platoon, commanded by Lt (QGO) Purandhoj Rai, and reported the situation
to Battalion HQ. By 1045 Lt-Col Fillingham, the Battalion CO,
had arrived at the foot of Track 6 in his scout car and after
speaking to Karamdhoj on the radio decided to send up reinforcements and attack without delay. About forty-five minutes
later Mayman and 1 Platoon joined the other platoon just below
the crest of the hill on Track 6. After a quick reconnaissance
Mayman ordered 1 Platoon to carry out a deep encircling movement which would bring them between the enemy and the
frontier, while 2 Platoon was to keep the enemy busy with a
feint attack from the front. The climax would be an assault by
1 Platoon from the rear.

Mayman had hardly finished giving out his orders when a
rifle shot cracked like a whip across the face of the escarpment
and echoed through the hills.

The section which, earlier that morning, had set an ambush
at the top of Track 6A had encountered the enemy. After a few
hours of inactivity Cpl Birbahadur Rai had decided to go forward
with two riflemen and observe the enemy positions. But the
enemy were much closer than he realized; the jungle was thick
and large rocky outcrops obscured the view. An Indonesian
concealed in a tree saw the corporal through the foliage. He
waited until the Gurkha was only six yards away before he

12. A Royal Artillery detachment's 105 mm Howitzer in action from a forward base near the Indonesian border.

13. HMS *Woolaston* on patrol up the Rajang River in Sarawak. The Royal Navy played a highly successful part in preventing the Indonesians from infiltrating terrorist groups along the 1,500 miles of coastline.

14. A patrol returns to base with native porters carrying rations and ammunition dropped by the RAF at a pre-arranged dropping zone.

fired. The bullet hit Birbahadur in the chest and killed him instantly. At once the two Gurkha riflemen returned the fire. A party of Indonesians crashed through the jungle in an attempt to charge them but at that moment the remainder of the section came forward from the ambush position and Rifleman Pancha-bahadur Rai's Bren gun hammered out an accurate and sustained fire, hitting at least two or three of the enemy.

The noise of the fight caused Mayman to abandon his original plan. A quick attack would now stop the Indonesians from escaping across the border. The Gurkhas moved rapidly up the hill, the two sections of 2 Platoon in the lead and 1 Platoon in reserve. At once they came under heavy fire from a hurriedly reinforced OP. The jungle was thick and the fighting soon became confused. Harassed by the Gurkhas' fierce and accurate fire the enemy fled, leaving one of their dead behind.

The leading section emerged from the jungle to find themselves at the foot of a sheer cliff with an escarpment to their left. From the top of the cliff the enemy kept up a steady fire. There seemed no possible way of moving forward so Mayman sent 1 Platoon round the right flank to attack from the rear.

No sooner had 1 Platoon disappeared, than Mayman discovered a route round the left flank by way of a narrow rock ledge which skirted the cliff, with a sheer escarpment below. He led the two sections along the ledge, inching along sideways while bullets screamed off the rockface.

The Indonesian commander realized that he was being outflanked and moved back under covering-fire from his machine guns. 2 Platoon pressed home their attack, advancing round the rocks and up into the main position. The Indonesians resisted fiercely but the Gurkhas eventually drove them back, inflicting several casualties. Immediate pursuit, however, was prevented by effective covering fire from yet another position sited further back along the ridge towards the border.

1 Platoon had started their attack at about the same time as 2 Platoon had begun theirs. Now, in the final stages of the action, 1 Platoon was making a right flanking attack to encircle the remainder of the enemy and cut off their line of retreat. The other platoon winkled out with grenades those left in the position. Shortly after 1600 the last of the enemy had withdrawn across the border. Five separate blood trails indicated serious

wounds, but the enemy had taken their dead and wounded with them.

The Indonesian commander had sited his camp in an exceptionally strong position, and had covered his withdrawal well, using the high ground to advantage. It was obvious that his men were regulars; the equipment left behind reinforced this conclusion. A nominal roll identified them as a platoon of 328 Raider Battalion, some forty strong. It was learned later that five had been killed and eight wounded, some of whom died.

A postscript to the battle occurred the following day when a radio message from the retreating raiders was intercepted: 'We have a lot of dead and wounded and are in considerable difficulties.' The reply from their headquarters was short and savage: 'Get on with it—there are plenty more where they came from.'

Following the action at Track 6, the Indonesians withdrew their forces from the Kling Kang Range with the exception of new positions some twenty miles to the east inside Sarawak. There, on a large hill opposite the longhouse at Kluah, which was friendly to the Security Forces, a unit of eighty Chinese and Javanese regulars and volunteers were encamped in three areas.

From these positions the Indonesians could easily observe all Security Force movement by foot, road, or river, so it was vital to dislodge them. As they were still in Major Mayman's area, A Company of the 2/10th Gurkhas was given the job, but this time they were to be assisted by supporting fire from the air and the ground. 845 Squadron had returned to the Second Division, and its Wessex helicopters were equipped to fire missiles. In addition, a troop of 105 mm guns from 70 Battery, RA, and two Saladins from The Queen's Royal Irish Hussars now came under Fillingham's command.

On 24 March, a terrorist abducted a Border Scout who was distributing leaflets up a track near the enemy camp. He was taken to the area and shown three separate camps to impress on him that the Indonesians could cross the border at will. Then he was released. The following morning he was telling his story to Mayman, and Operation Blunt was conceived.

For three days Mayman tried to pin-point the camps, but the more the Border Scout was questioned the more uncertain he became. The hill where the camps were located was featureless apart from a large rocky outcrop and was cloaked in thick jungle. Reconnaissances were made by air and from the ground but the exact location of the camps could not be established. Four days slipped by with nothing gained and Fillingham feared that the increased activity in the area might arouse the enemy's suspicions. He decided that the attack must be launched by 31 March, at the latest.

His plan was simple. First, two Wessex would fly over the target area each releasing a missile. Five minutes later the 105 mms would range. This procedure was to be repeated three times. Following this A Company would climb the hill covered by the 105s and the 76 mms of the Saladins.

A minute before H Hour at 0930 the first Wessex was poised at 2,000 feet waiting to discharge its missiles. Meanwhile, the guns had registered and were soon on target. As A Company started its advance the gunners increased their range. Climbing up the hillside the company had reached halfway when firing broke out from the top of the hill, but it was midday before the first enemy camp was discovered. Although it had suffered a direct hit from the 105s, it had unfortunately been abandoned some days before. The company continued its climb and about fifteen minutes later the leading platoon came under fire when approaching the second camp. The Gurkhas charged at once. Only two enemy were actually seen, one of whom was killed. The camp had been hit by the artillery but not by the missiles and the enemy had left in haste though with most of their equipment. The last camp, with room for thirty men, was found two hundred yards further on but this too had been recently evacuated.

When Fillingham decided that 31 March was the latest date for Operation Blunt he had another reason in mind. He was expecting an Indonesian incursion in the vicinity of Jambu and the Uli Ai River at the other extremity of the battalion area, and a battle there could not be controlled simultaneously with operations in Kluah.

During early March a large party of raiders, estimated at two hundred and forty mixed regulars and volunteers, had moved into the Uli Ai area north of Jambu. Following a report by Ibans, Major Tony Benn deployed his B Company into the area to search and attack. But the enemy had moved the previous day, some ninety going east across the border and the remainder, mostly irregulars and porters, heading south towards their original base. The company had bad luck in that the Ibans who had reconnoitred the enemy camp were captured. The Gurkhas did not reach the vicinity of the camp until last light and could do nothing until morning; the enemy moved out before dawn and were missed by twenty minutes.

It was evident that a further incursion would be made. B Company therefore remained concealed in the positions they had occupied since 10 March while C Company moved out of Jambu to the border area, poised to close in behind should the enemy try to cross the border.

This was the position when Fillingham arrived back in his headquarters at 1700 after Operation Blunt had been completed. At once he was called to the Operations Room to speak to C Company Commander on the radio. The Indonesians had crossed the border north of Jambu and were heading north-west towards B Company. Fillingham was delighted. He set off 'hot helicopter' for Jambu. Operation Sabre Tooth had begun.

Towards the end of March, Major Audy Patawari of the TNI led his thirty-six strong company of The Black Cobra Battalion across the border into the Lubong Tanah area of the Second Division. A few days later C Company found their tracks, and like mongooses the Gurkhas were soon on the trail of the Black Cobras.

The country was more favourable to the Indonesians. The going was exceptionally difficult with razor-back hills covered with thick, and in places impassable, primary jungle. Only near the longhouses were there cleared and cultivated areas. The tracks ran mainly along the line of the hills, and as there were few flat ridges these were like switchbacks and were always slippery from the daily rainfall. The conditions made it necessary to deploy more troops. Taking a justified risk, Fillingham left the rest of his battalion area, some one hundred and fifty miles in length, in the charge of A Company and a token force, and brought D Company under Major John Roberts, the Recce and Assault Pioneer Platoons, and the Gurkha Independent Parachute Company under Major Phillips into the Jambu sector.

The search continued through the early days of April until, on the 5th, an Iban hunting party was fired at, establishing the enemy's exact position. Fillingham moved C, D and Para Companies in behind them and closed the exit routes south and east. Meanwhile B Company increased their ambushes and remained in position. Between 6 and 7 April Fillingham put a deception plan into operation. This involved dummy helicopter lifts, the dropping of small parties at tactical points to stimulate fire, the helicopters' Brownings raking the areas not covered, and intermittent night firing by B Company. The plan worked. On the 7th the enemy turned and fled into the arms of 8 Platoon.

The Cobras had rested on a hill track while three men went forward on a reconnaissance. The Gurkhas held their fire until almost trodden on, then killed two of the scouts while the third went crashing down the hillside, severely wounded. The main body of the enemy fled leaving thirty packs, nearly all their food, and a considerable quantity of arms, ammunition and equipment. Split into small parties, the Indonesians went north again, joining up that evening at a rallying point. They then made another dash for the border only to bump into persistent 8 Platoon again. This time the Gurkhas held the initiative and throughout the remainder of the action like snake-charmers they made the Black Cobras dance to their tune. The unfortunate Indonesians were without food and short of weapons. Their leaders, who alone knew the country and had compasses, deserted them to make their own way back to base.

By quick helicopter lifts, platoons were moved into position to bar further attempts to break out of the ring. Four more contacts were made over the next three days and seven Indonesians were killed. A party of fourteen moved in sheer desperation to a cultivated area in search of food and were seen by a local Iban. The Iban rushed back to his longhouse where a Sergeant-Major of the Sarawak Police Field Force was enjoying a spell of leave. At once the Sergeant-Major gathered some twenty Ibans and set off in pursuit, catching up with the enemy, killing six and capturing seven. Only one escaped, and he almost certainly died of starvation in the jungle.

On 12 April a lance-corporal and a rifleman of B Company, were moving between ambush positions when they were themselves ambushed by four Indonesians. The two Gurkhas dived for cover as rifle bullets whined down the track and a grenade exploded among the trees. After the first fusillade the lance-corporal stepped calmly back onto the track and picked off three of the Indonesians, while the rifleman dispatched the fourth.

As a parting shot, C Company killed two more Indonesians near the border and the operation closed with a total of seventeen killed and seven captured. It was learned subsequently that three more had died later from their wounds. This accounted for twenty-seven of the original thirty-six. Throughout the operation the Gurkhas worked over desperate country, and only soldiers with high morale and in first-class physical condition could have succeeded as they did.

Platoons made forced marches throughout the night to reach positions in time to cut off the enemy. Many lived on one meal a day to avoid supply by helicopters which would have given their positions away.

'An onlooker,' said Fillingham later, 'might get the idea that a sledge-hammer was used to crack a nut. This is true relating to the deployed strength of the battalion to that of the enemy. But in jungle country of this nature, with the sanctuary of the border never more than two or three miles away, there is no alternative. The real key to success, however, was good shooting and physical fitness. In jungle warfare a target usually only presents itself for a brief moment. In Operation Sabre Tooth the ratio of kills to contacts, that is enemy actually seen and fired at, was one hundred per cent. Of eleven enemy shot at by men of the Battalion, ten were killed and one wounded who subsequently died.'

FOURTEEN
Ambush and Pursuit

The end of the January Truce also saw more Indonesian activity in the First Division where there were three major incursions during February and March 1964.

On 27 January 42 Commando embarked at Singapore aboard the MV *Auby* for a further tour in Borneo. The *Auby*, owned by the Straits Steamship Company, had been a coastal and river vessel conveying anything from deck passengers to cattle between Singapore and Borneo and up the wide jungle rivers. After a hasty conversion this was to be her maiden voyage as a troopship.

The *Auby* berthed at Biawak oil jetty and the Commandos deployed by road and helicopter to relieve 40 Commando. Almost at once Operation Dragon's Teeth was started. A party of thirty to forty IBTs had crossed the border into the Lundu District and headed for the Gunong Gadang, a towering feature overlooking Lundu itself. They had instructions to lie low and await further orders and were supplied with food and information by local Chinese farmers.

L Company 42 Commando, with B Company 1/2nd Gurkhas under command, set off in pursuit. A deadly game of hide-and-seek developed, with the Indonesians moving camp frequently. The aim was to deny the raiders food and this was achieved by breaking their system of contacts. Although short of food the Indonesians showed a commendable fighting spirit when they attacked a small Marine patrol killing the corporal in charge and wounding the other four.

By the end of Operation Dragon's Teeth five Indonesians had been killed, seven wounded, and four captured including the platoon commander, a regular army NCO. The remainder of the group had probably recrossed the border but there was a chance

115

that they had moved into the Sempadi Forest Reserve—the area between Lundu and Kuching.

Within a few days reports came in of strange lights to the north of L Company's post at Rasau. The hunt developed into a paper chase as the forty to fifty strong enemy party discarded ration packets and sweet papers in their wake. Unaccounted-for tracks led north across the Batang Kayan and into the Sempadi Forest. A mixed force of Marines and Gurkhas, led by Lt Ashdown and Lt Kakraprasad, crossed the Batang Kayan in pursuit. An enemy camp was located on 6 March but as the sections were deploying for the attack an IBT broke camp to fill his water bottle and had to be shot. With surprise lost a brisk battle followed in which the enemy withdrew in small parties leaving behind one casualty and a ton of equipment, weapons, and ammunition. Several more were believed to be hit, and it will probably never be known how many died in the jungle without food or medical supplies. For several days after the action Dyaks found bodies in or near the river, some of which showed signs of wounds.

A third major incursion was reported on 21 March when tracks were found in the forest near Lundu. Sgt Howe of 42 Commando was flown in with his tracker team to investigate. A tracker team consisted of a Team Leader (officer or sergeant) two Iban guides, a tracker dog and handler, an infantry patrol dog and handler, a signaller, and four cover men.

Howe and his team were soon on the trail of forty Indonesians. Following close, the tracker dog failed to point until too late and the enemy camp was bumped without warning. An hour-long fight ensued in which the Indonesians used light mortars. The Marine patrol became separated but disengaged successfully by nightfall. How many casualties the Marines inflicted could not be accurately assessed, but reports came in of wounded IBTs making their way homeward. A group looking for food was discouraged when one of their number forced an entry into a basha and the householder used his shot-gun to good effect.

During these weeks K Company 42 Commando was stationed in Bau District. In addition to Marine posts, a Malaysian Police Field Force post was under command at Tringgus in the south of the district. On the night of 21 February an Indonesian raiding party crept close to the defences of Tringgus in pouring rain and hurled in grenades, killing two policemen and wounding six. The police fought back and killed several of the enemy who withdrew across the border.

The police had their revenge on 29 February when they killed four Indonesians who walked into an ambush. Two more surrendered to 2 Troop. A patrol from 3 Troop surprised the enemy in a camp and killed five. During the next few days several Indonesians, weak and starving, surrendered to K Company. The *coup de grâce* was inflicted by a loyal headman when he shot two IBTs who had come in search of food.

The Commandos' vigorous action dampened the Indonesians' ardour and there were no more major incursions in the Bau area for the time being.

The threat to internal security was still ever-present and anti-CCO work continued ceaselessly. Although largely the responsibility of the police, the Security Forces were still called in to assist on several occasions. In the Bau District a cordon and search operation at Musi included police, K Company of 42 Commando, and C Squadron of the 1st Federal Recce Regiment. Several suspects were arrested and some documents seized. On one occasion three Chinese of the CCO, obviously forming contacts with the Indonesian raiders, were killed by a patrol from Recce Troop when they failed to stop on being challenged.

In June, 1964, came the next attempt to find a peaceful solution to Confrontation when a summit meeting was arranged in Tokyo between the Tunku, Sukarno, and Macapagal. To clear the air for the meeting, independent Thai observers were sent to Sarawak to witness the withdrawal of Indonesian guerrillas into Kalimantan. But even while the conference was being arranged over thirty border incidents occurred in East Malaysia. One of these led to a remarkable ambush by the 2/2nd Gurkha Rifles.

Capt Don Quinn commanding A Troop, 70 Battery RA learned that a cock-fight was to take place near his camp that Sunday. The last time this happened some Indonesian soldiers had come over the border in civilian dress. Quinn had the feeling that they might try again, so he passed the word to Lt-Col Neill commanding the 2/2nd Gurkha Rifles.

On the night of Friday, 12 June, Neill detailed the Assault Pioneer Platoon under Lt (QGO) Nandaraj Gurung for the task. The platoon moved up to Batu Lintang and discussed the operation with Quinn. It was decided that there were two possible entry routes, but unfortunately there was only one platoon to deploy. Eventually they decided that the more easterly of the two tracks, where there were no longhouses, would be fired on by artillery on Sunday morning, virtually compelling the enemy to use the other route.

The Pioneer Platoon moved out at 0500 on Saturday, 13 June, taking the most circuitous route. The track twisted and turned through rubber and low secondary jungle with high ground to the east. That afternoon they reached the ambush area and Nandaraj spent several hours on a detailed reconnaissance. By 1700 the dispositions were completed and the men were in position.

At best the platoon had been expecting the odd Indonesian in civilian dress off to the cock-fight, but fifty minutes later a force of over fifty Indonesians approached down the track from the direction of the border. This was a well-planned incursion aimed at establishing a group inside Sarawak. There was no question of the ambush being set on or near one of the withdrawal routes agreed with Thai observers while the Tokyo Talks were in progress. Nor was it a party of withdrawing guerrillas.

Some distance ahead of the main body were two scouts who were allowed to pass unscathed to the far end of the ambush. Not until the leading Indonesian section had entered the killing ground did Nandaraj give the order to open fire. Immediately the enemy went to ground and a savage fight began in torrential rain; darkness was coming on quickly and visibility was very poor. Two Indonesians who had taken cover in the centre of the killing ground were particularly troublesome. In order to see them properly in the fading light Rifleman Resembahadur Thapa, Bren gun at the hip, left his position and doubled forward through the rubber trees which were being struck by burst after burst of enemy machine gun fire. He killed the two guerrillas, and then returned to his original position.

The enemy opened heavy fire from the left flank with automatics and a 51 mm mortar and then formed up to counterattack from that quarter. Nandaraj killed one Indonesian himself, and throughout moved calmly around his platoon, which consisted of young soldiers with only seven months' service, directing fire and re-siting positions where necessary, encouraging each man. He realized that the fire from the left flank was the main danger, and leaving two men to cover the ambush killing ground he redeployed his men to meet the counter-attack. Shouting encouragement he ordered volley after volley of rapid fire which poured down upon the Indonesians who, with a superiority of four to one, were now rushing forward through the thick scrub. Once again Resembahadur left his cover and from an exposed position sprayed all enemy movement with bursts from his Bren.

A ragged Indonesian withdrawal followed. At once Nandaraj called for artillery fire to prevent further counter-attacks which might otherwise have been mounted. The Indonesians broke and retreated across the border, harassed all the way by artillery fire. Nandaraj, however, kept his platoon in position until shortly before midnight, when he moved them back to another hill to the north in case of mortar fire or further counter-attacks. The platoon stood to all night. In the morning they went down to have a look, finding nine Indonesian bodies and the weapon of a further dead man who had fallen into the near-by stream and been washed away. Each Indonesian had been shot through the forehead! At 0815 E Company Commander arrived with two platoons and took over. Only then did the Assault Pioneer Platoon prepare a meal—their first in forty-two hours.

The Tokyo Summit 'Truce' continued with several incidents. Parties of so-called guerrillas were seen leaving by Thai observers but obviously these groups had been sent in only a short while before as they were in clean, new uniforms. On 20 June the talks finally broke down. Within twenty-four hours Confrontation had resumed—on a new pattern.

FIFTEEN
A Change of Target

In General Walker's view the Security Forces' role in Borneo was offensive rather than defensive. According to Walker's plan, the Security Forces must avoid being tied to static positions. The base, whether company or platoon, should be held by the minimum number of troops to ensure its defence. The remainder should patrol and dominate the area by day, setting up different ambushes each night so that the enemy would never know where to attack and where to avoid. In addition, 105 mm howitzers were dug-in singly along the frontier as part of a base to provide harassing fire by night on all the likely Indonesian crossing places and approach routes. The same tactics were adopted by mortar teams.

Until the failure of the Tokyo talks the Indonesians had to a great extent avoided attacking these mobile bases. After the talks they changed their tactics, choosing known bases and helicopter LZs as their targets. Within twenty-four hours of the breakdown of the talks about a hundred Indonesians attacked a Security Force base in the First Division.

Two platoons of the 1/6th Gurkha Rifles had arrived there on the evening of 21 June, after a ten-day patrol. The commander made the mistake of occupying an old base instead of a 'poncho' base (a temporary position); otherwise he might have inflicted heavy losses on the enemy.

Shortly after the Gurkhas had settled down for the night the Indonesians opened fire with rockets, mortars, automatics, and rifles. A tough four-hour battle developed in which five separate attacks were thrown in against the position. By the time the enemy had withdrawn over the border five Gurkhas were dead and five wounded. It is not known how many casualties the Indonesians suffered.

On 18 July, Indonesians again attacked a mobile base, this

time at Bukit Knuckle, manned by 5 Platoon, 1st Green Jackets, under Lt Miers. Shortly after 1900 Miers received a report that about an hour earlier, while on the way to fish on the border due south, a local had seen one hundred Indonesian soldiers moving in the direction of the platoon's post. At that time the platoon was standing to as a daily routine, so Miers kept them at the alert throughout the evening.

Some twenty minutes later a junior NCO, who was in charge of a part of the perimeter known as Sangar Alpha, reported hearing enemy movement about two hundred yards to the south-east. Neither Miers nor his men could see anything, but vague noises were heard. The night was dark with low cloud obscuring the moon and a ground mist filling the hollows and swirling about the trees. There seemed little doubt that the enemy were present and trying to work round the east flank to the high ground north of the base. Miers, however, was determined not to engage until he was presented with a good target, and he imposed absolute quiet.

Suddenly bursts of automatic fire and rifle shots shattered the night from across a stream to the south and east at a range of about two hundred yars. A radio in Sangar Alpha, and an LMG in the hands of a rifleman, were hit. At once every weapon in 5 Platoon returned the fire. Sporadic exchanges continued until an hour after midnight when the raiders recovered their wounded and withdrew to the south-west. The Green Jackets directed their fire in that direction and this marked the end of the fight. Shortly after dawn a strong follow-up element was flown into Bukit Knuckle and a tracker team quickly established that the tracks led back over the border. Two pools of blood, a splintered bone fragment, and a field dressing case indicated at least two casualties.

By now the Security Forces were geared to the new tactics. In the Bau District, Major M. Koe, commanding B Company, 1st Green Jackets, was expecting an enemy attack on his forward patrol base near Stass which was manned by 7 Platoon under 2/Lt P. G. Chamberlin and included a 3-inch mortar crew. As a counter-move he ordered 2/Lt Roberts to deploy 11 Platoon in a cut-off ambush approximately a thousand yards south of the base.

At 0230 on 31 July, a sentry from 7 Platoon saw the slender

beam of a pencil torchlight to the west of the village school-house. At once the south-west front of the platoon was engaged by an enemy LMG at about eighty yards' range. At the same time three 2-inch mortar bombs passed well over the top of the base to explode some one hundred and fifty yards beyond. All the fire appeared to be coming from west of the schoolhouse. The Green Jackets retaliated, firing 2-inch parachute illumination flares. The 3-inch mortar crew, using primary charges, dropped their bombs into a gully which ran about one hundred yards from the position. Chamberlin set off explosive devices, two of which failed to go off—he later found that the wires had been cut. He then called for previously registered DF tasks. The 105 mm shells screamed overhead but exploded too far forward. Chamberlin was in radio contact with Lt Aitken, the artillery officer, and the fall was adjusted to about one hundred and fifty yards from the perimeter.

The Indonesians continued with intermittent fire from west of the schoolhouse, but the area was now completely dominated by the British platoon. Around 0300 the enemy decided to move out and fired a white Very light. Their line of withdrawal took them to the south-east across the front of the schoolhouse. More parachute illuminations were fired but, unfortunately, the 3-inch mortar crew had started using WP bombs and the smoke obscured the view. The 105 mm howitzers, however, continued harassing the track leading back to the border.

Meanwhile Roberts and 11 Platoon were waiting expectantly in their ambush position, the third they had occupied during the last three consecutive nights. He had placed battery-controlled RAF flares, the ignition of one to be the signal for the ambush to be sprung. He had also laid down hand-grenade necklaces and *panjis*.

The fight near Stass alerted the ambush party and at 0412 a group of men approached. Soon Roberts was able to make out the forms of the enemy, estimating their strength at around thirty. He decided to spring the ambush when the rear element was in the killing ground. The Indonesians came along the track in single file at roughly three to five yard intervals and led by a man with a torch. They were jabbering in an excited manner.

At the front of the ambush line were riflemen with shot-guns and when the last of the Indonesians were approaching them, and with some ten in the killing ground, Roberts ignited the flares. In the flash of light the platoon's killer group fired fifteen seconds rapid, a vicious hail from Bren, SLR, SMG, and shot-guns. Roberts also set off the grenade necklace south-west of the track which accounted for one enemy. Others were seen to fall under the small arms fire. The only retaliation was a wild burst from an SMG and a few rounds from an Armalite rifle.

There was some movement in the killing ground and the Green Jackets sprayed the area again. Roberts then withdrew his platoon to a previously selected rendezvous on a hill about a hundred and fifty yards to the rear, and called down artillery and mortar fire on to the enemy's expected route over the border.

At dawn on the 31st the Green Jackets' Commanding Officer and the RMO flew into 7 Platoon's base. At the same time a dawn clearing patrol found an enemy body in the gulley west of the schoolhouse. At the ambush killing ground 11 Platoon found four Indonesian dead. There was also blood on the *panjis* to the south of the track where at least two enemy making their escape had fallen on the sharp, bamboo stakes.

Later it was confirmed that six Indonesians had been killed in the whole operation, including a lieutenant, a sergeant, and four privates from a regular Indonesian regiment. Five had been wounded and nine were missing.

Towards the end of 1964 Lt-Col Corran Purdon of the 1st Royal Ulster Rifles was able to write: 'The morale of the border peoples is noticeably higher now, and the flow of information about the enemy is improving also as a direct result.'

To counter this situation the Indonesians tried to step up their terrorist activities against the locals, and several attempts were made to murder headmen. On 22 August, two women in the Serian District of the First Division were working a new stretch of hill padi near the border. They were approached by a group of Indonesian soldiers who asked if there were any Security Forces in Tepoi.

'There are none,' the women told them.

'In that case look out!' the Indonesian commander threatened. 'We will attack the village tonight.'

Tepoi was, in fact, near a Security Force position manned by 11 Platoon of RUR under Lt Paddy Doyle, and a 1/6th Gurkha company commanded, as Purdon put it, 'by that magnificent warrior, Major Harkasing Rai MC and Bar'.

The locals reported to Harkasing and he promptly arranged a warning signal of empty tin cans tied to a string running from the longhouse to his trench. That night there was shouting and movement in the village and the signal was given.

Harkasing waited three minutes to allow as many of the enemy as possible to approach before he fired a Very light. Surprise was complete but it did not belong with the attackers. A party of some thirty Indonesians who had crept barefooted into the village, leaving their boots neatly lined up on the track, turned and ran down the quickest escape route.

Opposite this path, across a small river and on top of a steep hill, waited Cpl Deignan and a section from the Ulsters' platoon. When Deignan heard the pad of running feet he set off two electrically detonated flares. Four running men were lit up by the bright light and the section opened fire. One man fell, the other three went to ground using trees as cover and dragging the wounded man out of the line of fire. The Ulster gunner on the LMG fired controlled bursts when a target presented itself. An Indonesian Bren replied and two rifles cracked out from the trees. The flares died away and the firing faded with the light. From a distance a 105 mm howitzer joined in to harass the retreating Indonesians.

Morning found three enemy dead opposite Deignan's position. Tracker teams followed up to the border and it was obvious from the blood trails that more had been hit. It was not a successful night for the Indonesians. They had also attacked Bukit Knuckle again and the 1st Green Jackets had accounted for three killed and two wounded without loss.

Although the Indonesians were still getting the worst of the exchanges, it was noticeable that more and more well-trained regulars were being used. They were prepared to ambush the Security Forces and to counter-attack. The day of the volunteer was passing rapidly; the new insurgent was tough and dedicated.

On 29 August, 1964, C Company of the 2/2nd Gurkhas, under

Major J. J. Aslett, was returning from an unsuccessful ambush. The point section of 10 Platoon came out of a patch of secondary jungle on to a track leading from the border. At that moment they entered the killing ground of an Indonesian ambush. Point-blank fire raked the leading Gurkhas. The number one of the LMG group was killed and his number two shot in the stomach. Bullets struck the section commander in the chest and knees, knocking him spinning; another NCO was shot through the head.

It is typical of Gurkhas that when all hell bursts loose around them there is nearly always one man who can save the situation. L/Cpl Amarjit Pun rushed forward through a hail of lead, put down his SMG and seized the fallen Bren gun. As his hands closed around the gun, enemy bullets put it out of action so he promptly picked up his own Sterling again and turned it on the enemy. Disdaining cover he stood in the centre of the killing ground, fully exposed to rapid fire at ten yards' range. Yelling encouragement to his men and obscenities at the Indonesians, he emptied magazine after magazine into the enemy ambush position until the fire dwindled.

Major Aslett, until then pinned down with his point platoon, now rose to his feet, and ordered the platoon commander to deploy in order to block the enemy and stem the fire. A bullet clipped his arm as he moved back in full view of the enemy to contact the rear platoon commander and instruct him to attack on the flank. This quick recovery and fierce counter-attack drove the enemy out and across the border. At least three Indonesians were killed and two wounded. The Gurkhas lost two killed and three wounded. The courage and control of Aslett and Amarjit Pun had made the difference.

Although Confrontation was increasingly a war fought by company and platoon commanders, the colonels tried their best to join in whenever possible. One afternoon in September, the MMG Platoon of 1 RUR opened fire on some Indonesians in an OP some six hundred yards away. Two fell, while the remainder disappeared over the ridge some one hundred and fifty yards from the border. Another man was sighted moving across the shoulder of the hill at four hundred yards' range and was hit. By this time Lt-Col Purdon had arrived in a Scout helicopter.

He ordered the pilot to fly low over the area while he dropped hand-grenades on them. A small patrol was landed later and it found heavy blood stains leading back across the border. The colonel had been on target.

SIXTEEN

'The Jungle Belonged to Us...'

Towards evening on 5 October, 1964, General Walker was handed an immediate signal. He read:

'MONGKUS. A BATTLE IS IN PROGRESS IN THIS AREA BETWEEN 2PL 2/10 GR UNDER COMD 1 RUR AND AN UNKNOWN NUMBER OF EN. THE GURKHA PL WAS IN AMBUSH WHEN ITS BASE PARTY WAS ATTACKED AT 1630 HRS. PL SGT IN BASE PARTY HAS SO FAR HELD OFF ENEMY WITH ASSISTANCE OF 105 GUN FROM GUNONG GAJAK. BASE PARTY WAS LOW ON AMMO BUT AMBUSH PARTY HAS JOINED UP WITH IT AT 1845 HRS. HEL IS ATTEMPTING FREE DROP OF SAA. 5 PL 1 RUR IS IN AREA AND IS MOVING TO JOIN UP WITH GURKHAS IF POSSIBLE. BATTLE CONTINUES. NO OWN CAS TO DATE.'

The Mongkus longhouse was about two miles from the border in the First Division, and within the operational area covered by the 1st RUR. Purdon had just handed over command to Lt-Col Hugh Hamil. In Hamil's own words: 'I was thrown in at the deep end'. The day after he took over, the battle was fought at Mongkus.

Under command of the Ulsters was a Platoon of the 2/10th Gurkhas, led by Sgt Barmalal Limbu. As the Indonesians had recently visited the area around Mongkus, the Gurkha platoon was busy patrolling and ambushing the approaches to the long-house. On 5 October Barmalal was instructed to ambush a track some two thousand yards north of the longhouse. At 1330 a party of fourteen men moved off to carry out this task, leaving Barmalal and nine men in position some hundred yards south-west of the longhouse. The base group constructed an LMG position. Then, posting three sentries, the remainder moved near the river, which ran to the south a short distance away, to cook their evening meal.

Shortly after 1500 the seven men in the cooking area heard shouting from the direction of Mongkus. A moment later the sentry nearest the village ran up to tell Barmalal that the enemy were about to attack the longhouse. The other two sentries were called in, and the ten Gurkhas ran to their position on a slight elevation with open ground on three sides and thick scrub on the other.

At once the sergeant ordered fire to be opened on the enemy, whereupon the Indonesians changed their target from the longhouse to the Gurkhas. A machine-gun hammered out flanking fire while about fifty Indonesians from the 305 Infantry Battalion made a frontal assault. The cleared rubber gave the Bren-gunner an excellent field of fire and the result was spectacular. The Indonesians withdrew across the river having suffered heavy casualties.

The enemy, however, was in considerable strength, and Barmalal realized that they were encircling his position preparatory to making another assault. He re-established radio communication with his Ulster commander, informing him as best he could of the situation and his location.

Shortly afterwards the Indonesians made a second assault, this time from the south. Once again the open ground gave the Gurkhas a good field of fire and the enemy wavered. Their attack was pressed for about twenty minutes, reaching within fifty yards of the position, until the steady and accurate Gurkha fire proved too much, and they were forced to withdraw.

Although the Indonesians had been held in two assaults, Barmalal knew that the situation was precarious. There was still an hour before dark, the weather was bad, and it was unlikely that he could be reinforced unless the remainder of his platoon returned from the ambush. He was also anxiously watching his ammunition supply. His men, however, were cheerful and full of fight, having successfully beaten off two attacks without suffering any casualties. Most of the enemy fire had passed harmlessly over their heads.

The third phase of the battle began with heavy LMG fire from the direction of the scrub which provided the enemy with a covered approach. At once Barmalal asked for DF fire from the 105 mm howitzer which was within range some five miles to the north-west. Shellfire came down promptly but was never within seven hundred yards of the battle, though it no doubt gave the enemy some anxious moments and hastened their final withdrawal. Sporadic fire broke out from as close as fifty yards from Indonesians still in positions as a result of the second assault. The Gurkhas replied with their 2-inch mortar. Then the third and final assault was launched, heralded by heavy covering fire including light mortars, but the bombs fell on their own troops and helped keep them back. The mortars quickly ceased fire and the enemy crept forward again through the scrub and overgrown rubber. It became clear that they would soon be able to overrun the position by sheer weight of numbers. Barmalal daringly decided to advance to the far end of the scrub where the field of fire was better. Leaving the Bren to cover the flank, the sergeant and the remainder of his small party crept through the scrub towards the advancing enemy. Almost at once two Indonesians were met at very close range and dispatched. A long and confused fight ensued in the thick scrub. The eight Gurkhas made skilful use of hand-grenades and held their fire until they were presented with a certain target. With the Bren firing on the flank, grenades exploding all over the place, and short, accurate bursts of SMG taking their toll, it must have seemed to the Indonesians that there was a Gurkha behind every bush. Just outside the battle area the 105 mm shells continued to explode with nerve-racking regularity.

In the fading light the Indonesians withdrew to the river line from where they kept up sporadic fire. The ten Gurkhas collected themselves together and took stock. Miraculously no one had been hit although some equipment had been shot off a few backs and water-bottles and jungle hats were riddled with bullet holes. Attacked by up to eight times their number, the Gurkhas had been victorious because of the fine leadership of their platoon commander, their own determination, accurate shooting, and aggressive action during the final stages of the battle.

They were down to an average of ten rounds per SLR and fifty for the Bren. All the hand-grenades had been used and no bombs remained for the 2-inch mortar. Repeated efforts were made by helicopters to drop ammunition to the Gurkhas but these were unsuccessful because of the failing light. Just before nightfall, however, the ambush party rejoined Barmalal, having evaded the encircling enemy and their own artillery and the position was thus made secure.

The Indonesians kept up a desultory fire until about 2100

when a heavy rain storm broke. With this they finally withdrew over the border, and for the time being peace returned to Mongkus. As usual the Indonesians carried away all their dead and wounded, but from the patches of blood and blood trails it was obvious that they had suffered heavy casualties.

'The jungle belonged to us,' said General Walker. 'We owned it—we dominated it—we conquered it.' Domination of the jungle was one of the important principles the General applied in his campaign. The lesson to be learned is that guerrillas, unlike conventional forces, do not lose wars if they fail to win them. They remain intact until the enemy tires. Accordingly, Walker determined that the guerrillas were to be denied the least respite. The Security Forces lived like guerrillas, played the enemy at his own game and out-manoeuvred the insurgents in every aspect of guerrilla warfare.

'We could never have achieved the results had we merely attacked and then returned to base,' Walker said later. 'Our object was to dominate and own the jungle week in, week out, day and *night*.'

The General took every opportunity to remind his commanders at all levels that the tactics should be 'secure and then hold' not merely 'search and destroy'. He also insisted on rigid security; forward troops were never allowed in any shop, café, or bar but rested in their firm bases away from the bright lights. The domination of the jungle was aided by the principle that in jungle warfare there can be no front in the accepted sense. So the security of bases did not present an acute problem. Everyone was responsible for his own protection; every man in uniform was a potential front line infantry soldier. The same rule applied to civilians, with every man his own vigilante. Only in this way was it possible to conduct a successful offensive defence and avoid tying up troops in static defence. 'I wanted to have more teeth in the mouth and less length of tail,' said Walker.

By relentless patrolling and aggressive ambushing day and night the Security Forces seized the initiative. It was essential to win the ambush game—this was the unwritten law of the jungle, an axiom made evident in Burma during the war against the Japanese. Since the end of this war, the spread of guerrilla warfare through many parts of Asia had accentuated the importance of the ambush, indeed, raised it to a near art-form. There were few large-scale battles; these were wars which could be won only by skilful patrols and ambushes. Constant success in this tactic lowers the enemy's morale. Like the repeated body blows of a boxer sapping his opponent's stamina the ambush rapidly demoralizes the enemy till he sees an armed figure behind every tree, takes cover at every sound in the jungle, and finally is reluctant to venture too far from his positions.

The importance of the ambush in Confrontation reached a peak in jungle warfare. It was one of the most effective means of dealing with the Indonesian raiders—striking them on the way in and on their homeward journey. Borneo itself was ideally suited for the ambush; a country of dense secondary jungle, rivers lined with deep foliage, primary forests, narrow tracks hugging cliff faces, and countless streams. For centuries the local people had ambushed game for the pot, or an enemy whose head was desired; standing for hours, blow-pipe ready, lips shaped to blow the deadly poisoned dart, as still as a tree, almost a part of the jungle. Now friends from abroad were using the jungle to stalk the enemy from across the border, but applying the same principle as the native hunter, waiting for hours or days—machine-gun or shot-gun ready, finger poised on the trigger—still as a tree, almost a part of the jungle.

The Security Forces reached a pitch of deadly efficiency surpassing even the Burma War standards. The twelve-year Emergency in Malaya during the late forties and the fifties—a guerrilla war of continual ambush and patrol—had provided considerable experience for many of the older soldiers serving in Borneo. Most of the officers and NCOs had been in Malaya and were experts in the art of ambush. They imparted their knowledge through tough training courses, and personally led many of the actions in the field. From first-hand experience they knew the importance of physical fitness. You had to be physically fit to endure the strain, waiting silently, patiently, seeing the same narrow patch of jungle track within your limited horizon, minute after minute, hour after hour, and still be alert when the enemy at last entered the killing ground. Then you had to fire quickly and accurately. That first fusillade was the most important; the moment of surprise would pass in an instant and the uninjured enemy could throw themselves to the ground and roll away into a position from where they could start shooting back.

Before climbing into the helicopter to be flown forward to the patrol zone, most battalions had standing orders that the men should have range practice to make sure that their weapons were working efficiently and the sights were properly aligned. The NCOs would make certain, too, that none of the men had applied a strong smelling hair oil, or drunk rum recently or smeared on any mosquito repellent. To an alert and expert enemy these alien odours could betray an ambush position as obviously as a rifleman accidentally firing his gun before the ambush was sprung.

In a country where it seemed that every bend in the track, every clump of bamboo, was a suitable place for an ambush, it was still essential to select the right spot with care. Only experience made this possible. An ambush commander, fussy in his determination to spring a successful trap, often took several hours making up his mind. Sometimes he would put his men in position, and then feel that the place was wrong, and move again to another spot. The commander had to be certain that the killing ground was the best—this was the area where heavy fire-power would be concentrated to kill as many as possible of the enemy who had entered the trap. A killing ground could cover anything from a few yards to several hundred yards depending on the number of troops involved. The commander would wish to make sure that any who escaped the first blast of fire-power would find it difficult to roll up the ambush—that is to counter-attack down the line of waiting men, catching them wrong-footed. There had to be good natural cover, field of fire, and line of withdrawal. When the right spot had at last been found, the troops would settle down to wait.

There was no set rule as to who should spring the ambush. More often than not, the troops would be positioned in groups of three or four, and the commander of the group covering the killing ground could well give the initial order. Usually the groups were in contact with each other by means of string which could be tugged to alert them of approaching enemy when sighted. At night the ambush commander would probably spring the ambush by setting off flares. The principle was to let the enemy scouts through, allowing the main body (so often not alert, looking down at their feet) to enter the killing ground before opening fire. Sometimes the enemy came from the 'wrong' direction, and ambushes were often set so that they could be sprung from either direction. The duration of the ambush and the number of men involved varied considerably and depended on the tactical situation. The mission might be to ambush obvious routes across the border as routine tasks, or to act on information which pin-pointed a route to be used by a force of Indonesians, or to set an emergency ambush, speeding out in helicopters which roped down the Security Forces behind the enemy and cut them off from the border. Sometimes the troops would remain in ambush during daylight hours only, returning to a patrol base at night. At other times they would stay in ambush for days on end, unrelieved. This was a nerve-racking experience. Silent, feeling quite alone and isolated from friends, although probably only a few feet apart, performing natural functions on the spot, this type of ambush really called for a high degree of physical fitness. And at the end of several days riveted to one uncomfortable jungle strip they had to be able at an instant's warning to shoot straight.

Affecting every ambush was the lie of the land. There was secondary jungle, which resulted from the habit of the local people of settling an area, burning and clearing the jungle, planting their rice, and moving on again. When they left the jungle returned thicker than before; the trees smaller but growing shoulder to shoulder, a dense tangle of undergrowth, lianas corkscrewing up the trees—the sort of country where troops had to cut a path, or follow the tracks and risk being ambushed. Then there was the primary jungle, with tall trees further apart, rising some two hundred feet, reaching out for the sunlight. Beneath the towering trees lies a shadow world, pierced by shafts of sunlight. For the soldier waiting in ambush it is like waiting in a cathedral; the buzz of the insects sounds like the murmur of sightseers on a guided tour round the cathedral floor. The jungle is intensely, brilliantly, green; most of the flowers— the fabulous orchids—grow high above in the treetops, and the soldier has no time to think about them, no time to climb into the upstairs room of the forest and search for the hidden botanical wonders. He moves on the ground floor. He approaches the ambush site through bamboos and through rattan palms ringed with fronds, attractive to the eye but armed with vicious hooks that tear uniforms and leave their mark on bare skin. Dark pools appear suddenly behind the undergrowth curtain, then are passed as the soldier wades through and melts again into the curtain on the other side.

There is the higher forest where moss smothers everything like a spongy green carpet. In the high hills, cloaked with thick layers of jungle, the mist rises from the valleys in the mornings and encircles the mountain peaks in cloud-like smoke rings. Steep, narrow paths skirt the cliff faces and are ideal ambush spots to snare the enemy as he climbs wearily, catching his breath; there is hardly any room to escape the fusillade of bullets screaming off the rock face. Countless rivers and streams cut through the countryside and make excellent ambush sites. The rivers are banked by the dark, mysterious forest. Hidden behind the foliage, waiting for the enemy to paddle up in boats, the rifleman sees the life of the river continue normally; fish break the surface, kingfishers dart by in flashes of brilliant blue.

In ambush the soldier waits for the prey to come to him like the near-by pitcher plant patiently waiting for insects to be caught in the sticky fluid of its pipe-like stem. Around him are the sounds of the jungle. The drone of countless insects, the flutter of wings, the cries of apes and hornbills; nerves are further tautened by the sound of a startled deer crashing through the undergrowth or the rumble of a falling tree. In the evening cicadas set up their night-long cry—a shrill, endless sound like the hum of a radio signal; and at dusk there is the beat of flying foxes, stumbling over the tree tops, settling on the fruit trees.

The soldier waits in all types of weather. Sometimes torrential rain drums down, forms puddles of slush beneath his feet; the dampness rises and chills his body, the rain seeps through the gaps in his poncho cape. Sometimes it is heat, with sweat and the insects; mosquitoes whine, settle and bite; flies land on his skin and irritate, and the soldier can make no violent move to drive them away. A worse torment are the leeches that smell his blood and stretch expectantly towards him; long, emaciated in their desire until they find his flesh and begin to bloat on his blood. The soldier waits, silent and enduring.

Suddenly the enemy scouts appear, rubber-soled feet padding along the track, tense, wondering if there is an ambush near by.

They are allowed to move through the killing ground. The ambush party wait like statues behind the jungle cover. Then the main enemy group appears, in single file. For the first time the jungle seems overcrowded. Each soldier waits for the signal. His SLR or machine-gun or shot-gun is tucked into his shoulder, his finger on the trigger. He fires. The shots echo through the jungle. He keeps on firing, raking the enemy with bullets. The sound of the shots fill his head, he feels the power of the weapon in his hands, smells the sharp tang of the cordite. The enemy scatter. Some are on the ground, crumpled heaps. An injured man cries out in pain.

As abruptly as the ambush was triggered, it ends. The troops depart. The jungle remains. For a while patches of blood, empty cartridge cases, ejected shells, bloated flies, flattened places in the grass mark the site of the ambush. But soon the jungle blots out the evidence of the moment of violence and the ambush remains only in the memories of the living.

On 4 November, 1964, Major Robinson of B Company 2/6th Gurkhas ordered the Assault Pioneer Platoon and one section of MMGs under Lt (QGO) Tejbahadur Gurung to deploy from Bario to Pa Lungan. Robinson himself with 4 and 6 Platoons moved from Raan Magaan along the border ridge to cover the most likely 'gate' to Pa Lungan. At dusk on the 3rd he camped four hundred yards south of the crossing and sent forward a patrol under Sgt Amerbahadur Pun. In the clear mountain air the patrol could smell smoke but darkness and the nature of the country (the average height was 6,000 feet) prevented Amerbahadur discovering its source. He returned to report some three hours after dark.

The following morning, Robinson sent forward a lightly-equipped scout group which came under fire from an Indonesian position further north of the border ridge. The enemy fired about eight hundred rounds and appeared to have four LMGs, but scored no hits. The scouts withdrew and Robinson decided to attack.

Amerbahadur was ordered to bring his 2-inch mortars into action, but the high ridge was covered in thick jungle, and the Gurkhas had to cut down several trees to clear a field of fire while enemy bullets slashed the foliage around them. When a gap had been cleared in the jungle canopy the mortars began firing. The first bomb shot up through the opening, but the second hit a tree and exploded, wounding Amerbahadur. He refused to be carried back to the LZ four hundred yards away. 'There is still fighting going on, and all the men are needed at the front.' He struggled back to the LZ by himself.

With the Gurkhas pressing hard the Indonesians withdrew skilfully to a second position north along the border ridge. The two Gurkha platoons then advanced up to the second position and attacked along the ridge, forcing the raiders back further north to the main position. Robinson led a third attack and the Indonesians were forced to split into small groups to recross the border. Three Indonesians were killed and two wounded. One enemy body was found, which was an unusual achievement as the Indonesians detailed special troops to recover their casualties.

In another instance, early in 1965, in which Robinson was again involved, the raiders threw their dead and wounded down a hill. Under cover of fire another party collected the casualties and carried them to the rear. In spite of this Robinson again managed to bring back a body.

Like many battalions, the 2/6th Gurkhas turned their attention to building themselves new and more impregnable defences. Their forward area was probably the only one with fridges, beds with mattresses (officers only!) and hot showers. This was because the battalion was detailed for an extremely long tour and made every effort to achieve comfort. In fact some gunners from 4 RA remarked that they would rather be in Bario than Labuan—not only was there hot water, but the local cinema was capable of taking Cinemascope!

The 1st RUR also dominated their area, which resulted in good intelligence reports from the locals. On 10 November, 1964, two Dyaks were working in their gardens when they saw an Indonesian patrol south of Tebedu. Rushing back to their village they told a third man who took them at once to Capt Boucher who was in the area with a ten-man patrol from 10 Platoon. Boucher moved quickly to the village where he met up with Corporal Paul of the Border Scouts who led him to the spot where the Dyaks had seen the raiders. On the way, the Ulsters met another local Dyak who had been asked by the Indonesians for the best route to Tebedu. He had calmly put them on to a roundabout route in order to give himself time to contact the Security Forces. Even more important, he was willing to show Boucher a path by which the enemy could be headed off.

The Dyak guided the Ulster patrol to the cut-off point which virtually meant running three thousand five hundred yards from one mountain to another. The patrol came off the jungle path to join the track at a point where it crossed a small stream. Boucher sent Paul to examine the track for any sign of the raiders, while riflemen stood by to cover him. Meanwhile Boucher established radio contact with Company HQ.

Paul returned about five minutes later, and within seconds Cpl Labalaba, the section commander, signalled the enemy patrol's approach. The country was hilly and the thick jungle and high undergrowth gave a limited field of fire. Boucher only had time to deploy Labalaba armed with an SLR, himself armed with an SMG, the Bren, and a rifleman to cover the stream. The Indonesians approached in single file just visible through the tracery of the jungle foliage. Five were in the killing ground when Labalaba, who had the best field of fire, sprang the ambush. All five were seen to fall as he sprayed them with a burst from his automatic rifle. The remainder retreated into thick cover and returned the fire. Boucher called for DF and when the first round crashed into the jungle the firefight ended. Fifteen more men of 10 Platoon were flown in by helicopter together with a tracker dog and handler. The area was searched until near nightfall when the party returned to Tebedu. A more comprehensive search was made the next day along the enemy's withdrawal route. At least three Indonesians had been killed and two wounded.

SEVENTEEN
Togetherness

Artillery support improved considerably in East Malaysia during Confrontation. At the beginning there was the problem of providing sufficient guns along the 1,000 mile frontier. So few were they that field guns soon became a status symbol to the infantry company commander. The forward infantry company bases had 'grown up rather like Topsy', and some of them, if lucky, had a gun to help out. There were graphic accounts of guns firing over open sights, and cries for cannister shot. This led to the belief that the guns were deployed for company defence which was not the case.

The infantry bases were not static defensive positions but frontier patrol bases from which patrols could dominate the border areas. Guns were deployed forward singly or in pairs inside the bases '*à la Waterloo*' to give maximum and continuous close support to the patrols operating in the border area; to cover as much of the border and likely Indonesian approaches as possible; to provide whenever possible close DF to neighbouring patrol bases; and to afford protection for the guns.

When Lt-Col Lyon arrived in February, 1965, to take over the 4th Light Regiment, RA, he had to redeploy because four guns had been removed from Borneo. The resultant deployment of close support artillery was more or less proportional to the enemy threat on each brigade front. Roughly one regiment was based in West Brigade and one battery in each of the other three brigades. Two batteries of the Federation Artillery were also included in the dispositions. If all the guns had been deployed forward this would not adequately have covered the front. In West Brigade, where the threat was greatest, one gun per battery was held in reserve at short notice to be moved to any given point. They were either 'galloped' forward in one piece by Belvedere or Wessex helicopters; or 'cantered' in bits by

Whirlwinds; they even practised a 'trot' in smaller sections in Sioux helicopters of their own Air Troop.

'In some of the forward bases we went in for a "double bed" concept,' wrote Lyon. 'This was nothing exciting; it merely entailed making preparations to put up a second gun when this was required and available for a few nights.'

The Indonesians showed a healthy respect for the medium artillery shells. One round within five hundred yards was usually sufficient to silence their mortars. In view of this the 5.5-inch guns of the Medium Troop, 170 (Imjin) battery, although organized to fight as one troop in one location, were frequently split into single-gun posts and moved wherever suitable tracks existed. The improving road complex in West Brigade gave them more scope.

The deployment of a battery of 105 mm pack howitzers by single guns, each with Command Post staff, and at the same time providing a varying number of Forward Observation Officers, meant using all officers as FOOs and Gun Post Officers (GPOs). There were, however, not enough officers to go around. This provided an excellent opportunity to give warrant officers and, better still, sergeants and bombardiers, the chance of practical experience as GPOs and sometimes FOOs.

In June, 1965, Lyon was made Senior Artillery Officer, Borneo, being official adviser to the Commander Land Forces and responsible to him for the technical efficiency of all artillery in the area. He also had the task of commanding his regiment in West Brigade. This meant wearing two hats. The first hat suggested that his HQ should be in Labuan, but the other demanded his presence most of the time in West Brigade. His Regimental HQ was therefore located seven miles south of Kuching. Control of the area outside West Brigade he maintained by personal visits to all brigade commanders and all guns about once a month, and by a Borneo-wide artillery radio control network. The BRA/FARELF, Brigadier Fawkes, allowed him a free hand and never once interfered with the way the gunner battle was run.

In West Brigade the gunner battle was being fought over two hundred miles of frontier. If the infantry battle was a company and platoon commander's war, then the artillery war belonged to the battery commanders. The close support of sometimes complex operations in jungle demanded a high professional standard for initial planning and subsequent control during the operation. The co-ordination of gun movement, air supply of ammunition, air troop tasking, and a hundred and one other aspects of regulating operations was the responsibility of Lyon's Second-in-Command.

Togetherness was vitally important. Close co-operation of gunners and infantry men at all levels in this type of war was more than a textbook imperative. Lyon started a drive to integrate his gun command posts with the infantry command posts in forward areas. The value was obvious: communications came back to the one control point, and if, for example, the infantry patrol radio was put out of action by an enemy bullet, the FOO's set could be used—or *vice versa*.

One of Lyon's knottiest problems was the provision of FOOs. It was not unusual for battalions to have four large patrols out at one time, each requiring an FOO. For the gunners this meant a long, exhausting, and dangerous 'walk' lasting a week or more, a couple of days' rest, and then out again with another company. '4th Regiment has never had such slim and fit officers!' Lyon was soon able to observe.

Togetherness worked. Even one of the more independently-minded and sceptical Gurkha commanding officers was heard to say that the success of a particular operation was 'entirely dependent on the provision of gunner support'. The Gurkhas frequently presented gun detachments with *kukris* to show their appreciation for really close support. When the Australian Minister of War asked Lyon what evidence he had that artillery fire was effective, the colonel was able to tell him that the best evidence came from the 3rd Royal Australian Regiment. After a highly successful joint action in the Bau sector in which eighteen Indonesians were killed, the Australian patrol returned to base and bought the gunners far too much beer.

Between the gunners and the local Dyaks there was a different kind of togetherness. The degree of closeness was obvious from the fashion of wearing 'blood brother' beads, and the gifts of blow-pipes and parangs. To date no gunner had been seen with Dyak tattoos on his neck, but apparently there were several close shaves.

Togetherness with the air forces was also very important. 'It is difficult to imagine how we could have managed without our own troop of three Sioux.' On occasions the pilot had to fly for eight or nine hours at a stretch over thick jungle directing gun fire or act as part of an airborne command post. The RAF also gave splendid help. The close co-operation with the helicopter squadrons was first class, and gunners were seldom short of essentials.

The Indonesians were not the only enemy. In this strange land, thousands of miles from home, the gunners had to face several hazards in addition to enemy action. In the hot and humid climate cuts and grazes went septic and skin diseases were difficult to avoid. The rigorous physical and jungle training carried out by the regiment prior to their tour of Borneo paid dividends. Tinea and other skin diseases appeared after a month but were kept within reasonable proportions by installing hot showers in even the most forward bases, and by the liberal use of powder. The men who suffered most were those who were regularly on patrol, frequently up to their waists and above in water and swamps.

In the patrol bases the dug-outs were similar to the 1914–18 pattern although they were made more comfortable, airy, and cheerful by the imaginative improvisations of the forward troops. Unserviceable parachutes were used to line the roof and walls, and Lyon had never seen such strikingly provocative pin-ups. There were snakes in the bases . . . but these helped to keep down the rats! The attractive young bare-bosomed Dyak girls in the kampongs were also on Lyon's list of hazards. But everyone soon became accustomed to their topless dresses.

The main enemy was boredom. This was partially relieved by rotating the men, and by establishing a Regimental Rest and Recuperation Camp on a Hawaiian-type beach near Kuching. A variety of pets, including honey bears, snakes, pigeons, tortoises, and monkeys all played their part in relieving tedium.

Crumbling field defences had to be inspected almost daily. Rebuilding the sandbag emplacements was a continuous task, and unless frequently doctored they only lasted about two months. The one more or less permanent method, the gunners found, was to revet the emplacement with corrugated iron.

Torrential downpours, even in the dry season, lasted several hours and tested the drainage of the gunpits, command posts, and living dug-outs, but there was never any great problem in drying out.

Important support was also given by the armoured regiments. Although it was not always possible for them, because of the lack of roads, to play their usual role, they often improvised to a great degree in support of the infantry.

Towards the end of 1964, the 4th RTR, commanded by Lt-Col John Cowgill, arrived from the Yemen and soon adapted themselves to their vastly different surroundings. The road conditions were extremely difficult for armoured vehicles. The limited road network wound its way through hilly jungle-covered country, often skirting sheer precipices, and crossing numerous small bridges which could barely take the weight of the vehicles. Sudden and frequent torrential downpours turned the rubble surfaces into muddy, slippery mires.

In order to release trained infantry for border patrols, machine-gun teams from the RTR's Sarawak Squadron took over posts in the forward company locations, using the Ferret's .303 Browning in its ground mounted role.

Cpl Moore of 3 Troop was detailed with his driver to form a Browning machine-gun crew. 'My first impression of a forward location in Sarawak,' he writes, 'was that of an aerial photograph taken of the trenches and dugouts somewhere in France about 1917. The only difference was that on closer examination I found the troops dressed in more modern kit (if OG shorts are modern) and the difference in equipment.'

On 28 December, Moore and his driver reported to the 'Chopper Pad' at Bau, complete with Browning, ground mounting, ten boxes of ammunition, and personal kit. A fifteen-minute trip in an RAF Whirlwind brought them to the forward base, where they were taken on a guided tour:

'Although the area was very small, it was a mass of small underground passage-ways linking stores, offices, kitchens, canteens, living accommodation and weapon pits. I found that the 5ft 4in to 5ft 6in Gurkhas flew along the passage ways. I, being around 6ft, spent most of my time either on all fours, where some beam striking my head had put me, or with my head bent, creeping gingerly along.

'The Gunner accommodation, where we were living, was surprisingly comfortable and very secure, being down at least

10ft and with three layers of sandbags and timber overhead. The first evening we had a stand-to and the position opened fire with all arms. The noise and fire-power was very impressive, with the LMGs, and GPMGs plus our BMG as the automatic weapons.

'On our second day we had a supply drop from an R.A.F. Hastings and we noted the accuracy with which the aircraft dropped some 40 'chutes on to an area of about 50×25 yds. A few stray ones fell into the jungle and outside the wire, and these were quickly retrieved by the Gurkhas and local labour. The locals arrived from a Kampong some 500 yds away every morning ready to construct new pits and clear pathways as and when required; the mothers and children arrived about 9 a.m. to see the medical orderly, who acted as the local doctor. Any serious cases, whether they were servicemen or civilians, were flown out in a helicopter that called every morning.

'The old year out and the new year in was celebrated by the 105mm firing 21 rounds. Our "Jock" cook still insisted on "first footing" and was rewarded with at least two tots from the Gurkha operations room and sentry pit.

'The days seemed to pass very quickly and the nights very slowly. The 105mm fired nearly every night, and as our hut was only a few yards away from the gun, we would always wake up. The Artillery boys, not on duty that night, would sleep through all this quite happily, knowing that all was well.

'When we received word that we were returning to Bau we were disappointed. We had got quite used to the life and found it very enjoyable, but the thought of cold beer speeded us onward and, as we left by air at 5.30 p.m. on the sixth day, I again had the image of World War I entrenchments, and then realised how wrong first impressions can be. After all, who ever "first-footed" at the Somme?'

In the pale Singapore dawn, the crew of an Argosy from 215 Squadron, RAF, would drive through the deserted streets on their way to Changi aerodrome for the 1,500-mile flight to Borneo and back. Four or five times a week an Argosy of 215 Squadron flew this 'Milk-run', a vital part of the work of the RAF in the Far East.

RAF helicopters continued to give excellent support, often in hazardous conditions, as an incident which occurred in February, 1965, illustrates. On the morning of 28 February, an SAS patrol commanded by Sgt Lillico was moving through the jungle on the border when it made contact with the enemy. The Indonesians opened fire immediately and both Trooper Thomson and Lillico, the lead scout and second man respectively, were badly wounded. They returned fire, killing two Indonesians. Lillico ordered Thomson, who he thought could crawl, to return to the emergency rendezvous. He, himself, could hardly move as his legs were paralysed. However, he managed to drag himself out of the immediate contact area into some bamboo cover and then lost consciousness.

The following morning he came to and dragged himself some five hundred yards to the top of a near-by ridge where he hid in thick undergrowth. Shortly afterwards he heard a helicopter. The previous day, Flying Officer Collinson had flown from Kuching in his Whirlwind to search for the two wounded SAS men. By skilful flying and expert use of his radio Collinson picked up a signal from Thomson and established his most probable location. This enabled a ground patrol to contact the trooper.

The next day the pilot resumed his air search and found the stretcher party with the wounded man, but tall trees prevented him from bringing his helicopter in low enough for the winch to reach the ground. As he turned away he picked up a radio signal from Lillico's Sabre beacon, which the sergeant had switched on to attract attention. Almost at once Lillico heard movement in the jungle and caught a glimpse of Indonesian soldiers. On the approach of the helicopter, one of the soldiers climbed a tree some forty yards away to look around. Realizing that the beacon signal would bring the helicopter within reach of the enemy, the sergeant switched it off and crawled away to another hiding-place.

Later that day, Collinson returned to the area. By this time Lillico was far enough away from the enemy to switch on his beacon, and the pilot spotted him through the trees. The lie of the land presented a difficult task, but Collinson backed the Whirlwind's tail rotor between two tall trees, guided by his navigator, and positioned the aircraft so accurately that Lillico was able to attach himself to the strop and be lifted into the cabin. By now night was falling and Collinson flew in darkness, skirting a line of active thunderstorms, to land at Kuching. Next morning, Collinson returned and flew Thomson out.

EIGHTEEN
Sukarno's Second Front

In the early hours of 17 August 1964, a flotilla of small craft set out from Sumatra across the narrow Malacca Straits. In the boats were 108 Indonesian infiltrators, consisting of 53 Regular Airforce Paratroops, 21 Regular Marines, 32 Malaysians (of whom 27 were Communist Malaysian Chinese) and two Indonesian volunteers. The first major incursion into West Malaysia was under way.

Their plan was to land at three separate places each about eight miles apart on the coast of south-west Johore. One group of forty-five men would come ashore at the mouth of the Sanglang River near Benut, thirty-three would land at Pontian Kechil, and the remaining thirty at Kukup. Once ashore the groups would rendezvous on Gunong Pulai, a jungle-covered mountain twelve miles inland from Pontian Kechil, and there establish a guerrilla base for the training of dissident Malaysians. The men in the boats believed that the local population would welcome them with open arms and rally to the training camp in hundreds. Leaving a regular training cadre in the camp, the remainder of the force would then move up to the Gunong Blumut jungle area east of Kluang in central Johore, eventually to link up with an airborne force to be dropped near Labis in north Johore.

It was about 0600 when the Pontian Kechil group disembarked. They were quickly discovered and retaliation was swift. A near-by police post opened fire and the Indonesians scattered, abandoning a good deal of equipment. At once the alarm was raised along the coast. By the 23rd all but four of this group had been captured and the full extent of the invasion came to light.

The Benut group also ran into Malaysian forces within a short time of landing and lost four of their number. The remainder managed to reach the swamp jungle to the east of the cultivated

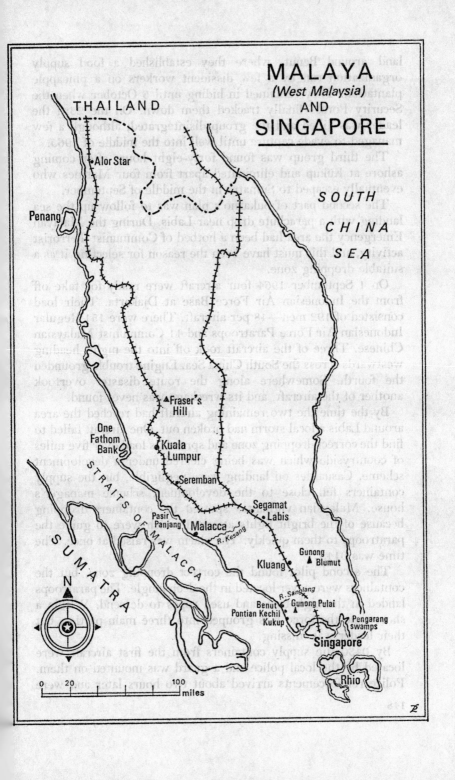

MALAYA
(West Malaysia)
AND
SINGAPORE

THAILAND

• Alor Star

SOUTH
CHINA
SEA

Penang

▲ Fraser's
Hill

One
Fathom
Bank

■ Kuala
Lumpur

S U M A T R A

• Seremban

Segamat
• Labis

Pasir
Panjang
• Malacca
R. Kesang

Kluang

Gunong
▲ Blumut

R. Senglang

Benut   Gunong Pulai
Pontian Kechil ▲
Kukup

Pengarang
swamps

Singapore

Rhio

N

0 20   100
└─┴──┴──┴──┴──┘
miles

land around Benut, where they established a food supply organization run by a few dissident workers on a pineapple plantation. They remained in hiding until 6 October when the Security Forces finally tracked them down. On the 23rd the leader was killed and the group disintegrated, although a few managed to evade capture until well into the middle of 1965.

The third group was found forty-eight hours after coming ashore at Kukup and eliminated apart from four Marines who eventually escaped to Sumatra in the middle of September.

The second part of Sukarno's plan was to follow up the sea landing with a parachute drop near Labis. During the Malayan Emergency the area had been a hotbed of Communist Terrorist activity, and this must have been the reason for selecting it as a suitable dropping zone.

On 1 September 1964 four aircraft were ready for take off from the Indonesian Air Force Base at Djakarta. Their load consisted of 192 men—48 per aircraft. There were 151 Regular Indonesian Air Force Paratroops and 41 Communist Malaysian Chinese. Three of the aircraft took off into the night, heading westwards across the South China Sea. Engine trouble grounded the fourth. Somewhere along the route disaster overtook another of the aircraft, and its wreckage was never found.

By the time the two remaining aircraft had reached the area around Labis a local storm had broken out. One aircraft failed to find the correct dropping zone and spread its load over five miles of countryside which was being cleared under a development scheme. Casualties on landing were negligible, but the supply containers fell close to the development scheme manager's house. Malaysian vigilantes spotted the containers dropping because of the bright lights attached which were to guide the paratroops to them quickly. The alarm was raised at once. The time was 0145.

The second pilot found the correct dropping zone, but the containers were never located in the deep jungle. The paratroops landed in the high trees and used ropes to descend. Within a short time the force was grouped into three main parties, but their leader was missing.

By 0430 the supply containers from the first aircraft were located by the local police and a guard was mounted on them. Police reinforcements arrived about two hours later and were soon in action when they bumped into the paratroops who were still searching for their containers. The Indonesians scattered, leaving behind some casualties. The location of the second group was not known at this time, however, nor was the full strength of the invasion.

The Security Forces were alerted on 4 September, the 1/10th Gurkhas deploying in the Labis area, their old hunting grounds of the 1949 Emergency. Lt-Col Burnett established his Tactical HQ in the Labis Police Station. It was almost like turning back the pages of history to fifteen years earlier. 'Many old hands of the Battalion were there, only a little bit older, wiser and more rotund, but their keeness still not blunted. . . . Like terriers on a rat hunt, the Battalion converged on Labis and then scuttled off into the jungle on the scent.'

The 1st Royal New Zealand Infantry Regiment was also brought into the area, their camp situated in a palm oil plantation. To a grassy strip in the middle of the camp came half of 845 Squadron, rushed up from *Bulwark* and under the command of Lt John Morgan.

Labis was wild country split by the main motor road from Singapore to the north. Rubber plantations fringed the road, giving way to thick jungle and dense undergrowth. Movement was slow, but the routine of Borneo came into play with helicopters roping in search parties.

For a whole month Gurkhas and Kiwis hunted out the Indonesian paratroops. If the New Zealand battalion did not have the same success as the Gurkhas it was not for want of trying. To be fair, the Gurkha commanders, with their hard-learned knowledge of the area when fighting the Communist Terrorists, had the advantage.

On 7 September, A Company of the 1/10th opened the score with one killed and two captured. Three more were killed by C Company on the 9th. The pattern continued with more Indonesians being picked up every day. On the 13th the Gurkhas had their first fatal casualty when a lance-corporal was shot in an action in which four Indonesians were killed and seven captured.

On 22 September information about a party of Indonesians reached Burnett. He sent out a small group which contacted the enemy just before nightfall near an iron ore mine north of

Segamat. There was a brief encounter before the two groups lost contact.

The Gurkhas camped for the night, setting off at dawn with tracker dogs. It was two in the afternoon before they caught up with the Indonesians. Quickly they closed in, using grenades. Major Haddow was in the forefront, and saw movement ahead. He threw a grenade. With the sound of the explosion still echoing in the jungle, Haddow looked over the buttress of a big tree to see the effect and was killed at point-blank range by an Indonesian paratrooper. At this, Capt (QGO) Aitabahadur took over command, and the Gurkhas put in a fierce attack, killing all the Indonesians.

Many of the names on the Indonesians' order of battle became familiar to the Gurkhas, and a sense of satisfaction was felt when news was received that one of the more important figures had been killed or captured. One elusive character, to whom all Indonesian ranks kept referring, was particularly wanted: Sergeant-Major Wogimen. At the end of the battalion's part in the operation early in October 1964, the Gurkhas were forced to the regretful conclusion that Wogimen was still hanging from his parachute in one of the trees somewhere in the jungle.

On 29 October, fifty-two more infiltrators made a sea landing, this time at the mouth of the Kesang River on the Johore–Malacca state boundary. A number of fishermen saw them coming ashore and immediately reported to the local police station. Police, and men from the 3rd Royal Australian Regiment and the 1st Royal New Zealand Regiment formed a tight cordon among the mangrove swamps and fruit plantations. Within thirty hours, fifty raiders had surrendered. The remaining two were captured three weeks later in a state of exhaustion and near to starving.

Two more major attempts were made along the west coast. On 23 December twenty-eight Indonesians landed in south-west Johore. Within a short time they were cornered in thick mangrove swamps. Three were killed and the rest captured. On Christmas Eve sixty-one Indonesians made a longer sea crossing in an attempt to land north-west of Kuala Lumpur. The force was transported to an Indonesian island in the middle of the Malacca Straits by an Armed Customs Patrol Launch (ACPL). The launch pirated ten Malaysian fishing boats from One Fathom Bank off a Selangor fishing village to take the force on the next stage of its journey. But the convoy was intercepted by HMS *Ajax*. Seven fishing craft were captured with large stocks of ammunition and explosives although the ACPL managed to escape.

With their failure to land on the west coast, the Indonesians turned their attention to south-east Johore. Between 7 November 1964 and 25 March 1965 five attempts were made to establish guerrilla groups in that area. The first two attempts in November and December were soon blunted by the Security Forces. On 25 and 26 February forty-four Indonesian police and volunteers came ashore and at first achieved a successful ambush. They killed eight and wounded five from a platoon of the Singapore Infantry Regiment which caused Walker to remark: 'It brings home to everyone that no matter where they are danger is lurking in every area throughout Malaysia.'

By the end of March the Security Forces had accounted for all forty-four infiltrators. Two more landings were attempted in March, but these too came to a quick end. There were several minor incursions later, but no further major attempts. Perhaps word eventually got back to Indonesian command that there was little chance of gaining local support in West Malaysia. Interrogation of prisoners revealed that, right up to the end, the Indonesians sent on these trips were firmly convinced that Malaya was ripe for insurrection. It seems incredible that their commanders could have been of this opinion. A more likely explanation is that after the first abortive attempts, Sukarno's main reason for pursuing these tactics was to keep the Malays on edge.

NINETEEN
No Sunrise for Sukarno

In a National Resurrection Day speech in Djakarta on 20 May 1964 Sukarno had boasted that Malaysia would be crushed by the time 'the sun rises on 1 January 1965'. But his invasion of West Malaysia had ended in disaster, while in Borneo General Walker had demolished the first two stages of the guerrilla war. Sukarno had to revive the momentum of Confrontation and he ordered a considerable build-up of forces along the Borneo border, as well as in forward island bases flanking Singapore and the south-west of the Peninsula.

Towards the end of 1964 intelligence reports confirmed Sukarno's new strategy and Walker at once asked for reinforcements. Although he had so far successfully contained the guerrillas he never underestimated his enemy. He was determined to show the Indonesians that Malaysia meant business, and this had to be done from a position of strength.

The 1st Bn, The Scots Guards, recently arrived in Singapore, was ordered to Borneo; while from Britain, the 2nd Bn Parachute Regiment and the 3rd Green Jackets were moved at short notice—the latter bound in the first instance for Hong Kong to relieve a Gurkha battalion which would also be flown to Borneo. With the addition of 2nd Parachute Regiment and 3rd Green Jackets, the strength of British Far East Land Forces, including Gurkhas, was increased to about eighteen battalions: two Royal Marine Commandos, eight Gurkha battalions, and seven to eight British. In addition, the Malaysian Army consisted of eight battalions, half of these in Borneo. There were also two battalions of the Singapore Regiment in Singapore. The Commonwealth Brigade, of some eight thousand Australians and New Zealanders, was in Malacca but had not as yet been used in Borneo.

More ships joined the Far East Fleet. Four minesweepers and

two seaward defence vessels in 'mothballs' at the Singapore naval base were reactivated for patrol work in West Malaysian territorial waters. The Far East Fleet consisted of about eighty vessels. In fact with the aircraft carriers *Victorious* and *Centaur*, the Commando ship *Bulwark*, and the guided missile destroyer *Kent*, the fleet was larger than at any time since Korea.

The RAF V-bomber Squadron was reinforced with more aircraft. An extra squadron of Javelin all-weather fighters and the latest type of Bloodhound Mark II defence missiles were put into the area.

In Borneo, responsibility had originally been divided between three brigades: West, Central and East. Their frontages were 623, 267 and 81 miles. The longest battalion front was 382 miles—in the Third Division. It was decided to break West Brigade into two: West and Mid-West. The brigade fronts then extended 181, 442, 267 and 81 miles. The main battle area, however, continued to be the First and Second Divisions with their correspondingly greater concentration of Security Forces.

South-west of Pensiangan the Indonesians tried probing attacks along the Fifth Division border. Late in January, 1965, about fifty raiders crossed the border and took up a strong defensive position in the hills which rose to eight thousand feet in places. Because of the difficult terrain little was known of the enemy's strength and weapons. But they had to be moved.

On 29 January, Capt Jackman, commanding C Company the 1/2nd Gurkhas, was ordered to attack. Jackman decided to carry out a night march prior to an assault at dawn to achieve maximum surprise. Because of the distance separating the objective and the company base, careful planning was required to ensure that the Gurkhas arrived on time.

After a hard night march along a switchback of twisting tracks through dense jungle, the company found the Indonesian camp before dawn. There was little opportunity for a reconnaissance which made the 3-inch mortar group's task especially difficult. Base-plate positions had to be selected in the dark and, of course, no pre-registration was possible.

As daylight spread across the hill-tops Jackman launched his attack. But he found that the raiders had withdrawn during the night to another position several hundred yards away, leaving only a small holding force in the original spot. The holding force was quickly dispersed but heavy fire fell on the Gurkhas from the new position. Two MMGs were particularly active, killing one Gurkha and wounding two. Cpl Birbahadur Gurung, in charge of the 3-inch mortar mobile fire control, realized that the machine-gun posts had to be put out of action as quickly as possible. But he was unable to locate them accurately. Regardless of the danger he stood up in the open in order to be able to give accurate fire orders to his mortars which quickly silenced one of the guns.

The Indonesians brought their own mortar into action, the bombs exploding dangerously close. Birbahadur directed his mortars on to the new target. The second bomb hit the enemy pit; there was a blast of flame which mushroomed as the enemy's own mortar bombs exploded, disintegrating mortar and crew. For more than an hour Birbahadur continued to direct his mortar fire, eventually silencing all the enemy's support weapons. At least eight Indonesians were killed and as many as thirty wounded.

The 1/7th Gurkhas continued to uphold their tradition in the Bau District, with constant patrols and ambushes to keep the enemy on his toes and think twice before daring to cross the border.

On 18 February 1965 Capt (QGO) Bharat Rai of the 1/7th set off on a patrol through dense jungle and in torrential rain to reconnoitre a track near the border. Three hours later the scouts heard men talking on the track ahead of them. At once Bharat ordered his fourteen-man patrol to advance more stealthily and the men reached to within five yards of five armed Indonesians. The Indonesians were crouched on their haunches in a cluster, studying papers and maps. It was obviously a commander's order group, but before Bharat could take any action he heard the sounds of about fifty men moving in the jungle off the track to both his right and left. He was in a dangerous position, and risked being surrounded and cut off. But the target ahead seemed too vital to miss.

Silently, he deployed his men into fire positions. The enemy commander rose to his feet, and stretched to loosen the stiffness in his thighs. The leading Gurkha scout immediately opened fire and the Indonesian commander spun and fell, the maps fluttering out of his lifeless hands. The remainder of the patrol blasted the order group with fire, killing three more and badly wounding the fourth. At this the enemy opened up with heavy automatics and rifles from both flanks. The noise was deafening and above the heads of the crouching Gurkhas a hail of bullets cut through the air and slashed the undergrowth to ribbons.

Bharat extricated his patrol, firing some parting shots at both flanks and wounding at least three more of the enemy. Some thirty minutes later the Gurkhas halted; in the distance they could still hear the Indonesians firing fiercely away into thin air.

March, 1965, saw the end of General Walker's tour as Director of Borneo Operations. It was a sad moment for troops and civilians. In those first years of Confrontation he had been the prime architect of the solid resistance built up by the Security Forces, and the instigator of the aggressive spirit which was apparent in all engagements fought against the Indonesians. He was a soldier's general, with the knack of endearing himself to the local people as well. It was due to his drive and determination above all that Confrontation had so far failed.

Before he left on 12 March, 1965, to become Deputy Chief-of-Staff (Operations and Intelligence) HQ Allied Land Forces Central Europe, Walker said, 'I have learned the immense value of helicopters, and the vital importance of training and equipping our soldiers for insurgency-type operations and guerrilla warfare in tropical climates.'

The new Director of Borneo Operations was fifty-three year old Major-General George Lea, who started his military career in 1933 when he was commissioned into the Lancashire Fusiliers. By the time he took over the guerrillas had virtually been smashed, and he was faced with a war on more conventional lines. It is always difficult to take over towards the end of a campaign; to do so from someone like Walker must have been particularly difficult. But if Lea was not as flamboyant as Walker, he had a quiet charm and determination of his own which was soon apparent in the months of fierce, company actions which followed.

It was clear, certainly, that Confrontation had reached its

final stage. The Indonesian commanders had more or less discarded guerrilla tactics and were launching their regulars in all-out attacks on the Security Forces' border positions. It was Lea's task to ensure that the regulars were broken on the border, and that the war did not escalate into total war. At the same time he had to make certain that a tight grip was still maintained on internal security.

In the final months of 1966, when Confrontation was dying on its feet, and politics demanded that nothing should be done to ruin the chance of peace, Lea had the added difficulty of keeping his own troops in check.

Shortly after Lea's appointment, the 2nd Bn, the Parachute Regiment, moved into Borneo on its first tour. Commanded by Lt-Col Eberhardie, the battalion established its HQ at Balai Ringin, a semi-fortified position some sixty miles south-east of Kuching. The rifle companies moved to their forward positions which they found had been hacked out of virgin jungle and consisted of static bases heavily fortified with sand-bags, bunker wire, Claymore mines, night lighting for illuminating fields of fire, and had both a radio link and communications trenches between strongpoints. The jungle immediately surrounding the positions had been cleared to give fields of fire and sown with wire, mines, and *panjis*. Each location had its own 3-inch mortar detachment and two of the companies had 105 mm howitzers within the perimeter. One of the companies had the additional fire-power of a detachment of 4.2-inch mortars.

All the bases were within two thousand yards of the Indonesian border, and patrols moved out from them for periods of anything between three and ten days. The only lines of communication to bases were airdrop or helicopter lift, and each company had its own DZ and LZ. In addition, roping areas were constructed in jungle across the battalion front to enable troops to be roped down in strength.

The battalion had been in residence only a few days when there were signs of enemy activity to the south of Plaman Mapu. Between 27 March and 6 April, B and D Companies reported incidents on their front including automatic fire and lights. On the 14th, D Company found signs of an enemy incursion of between fifty and sixty men in the area of Gunong Gajak. From litter and equipment recovered it was evident that the Indo-

15. The Security Forces operated in extremely difficult terrain. The Royal Ulster Rifles seek out the enemy in a deep, evil-smelling swamp.

16. Men of the Royal Ulster Rifles embarking in long-boats prior to a river patrol.

17. A patrol from the King's Own Yorkshire Light Infantry in a typical jungle setting.

nesians were in possession of 44 mm Yugoslavian M-57 rocket-launchers. This, plus the greatly increased activity in B Company area, confirmed that an attack was planned in the Plaman Mapu sector and would probably include rocket-launchers. The most ominous discovery was made on 12 April: positions had been cut out in the jungle overlooking Plaman Mapu for rocket-launchers or machine-gun mountings. Throughout 14 to 27 April enemy action was stepped up on all company fronts. The situation was rapidly coming to a head.

At about 1830 on 26 April, about a hundred men from an elite Javanese TNI battalion passed through Tembawang west of Plaman Mapu. Moving from west to east they probably took a route around the north of Gunong Rawan through the 1/6th Gurkhas' area. Another fifty entered Kampong Plaman Mapu from the east at about 2100. Two other companies formed a forward base and a rear base.

The Para company's position was vulnerable and overlooked by surrounding hills. On this night it was manned by a numerically weak platoon of young soldiers, B Company HQ, and a mortar section, the whole under command of CSM Williams. Realizing that the Indonesians were planning to make an attack some night soon, the platoon was very alert.

Behind the curtain of darkness the Javanese spent the early part of the night making a close approach. Then they formed up in a deep gully to the south-west of B Company's perimeter. A few minutes after 0500 on 27 April, two Very lights broke the darkness and at once a savage assault was launched. The blackness of the hour before dawn was split by sound and light as 44 mm rockets and 50 mm mortar bombs exploded in a fountain of earth and flame.

The Para platoon stood to within a few seconds which probably saved several lives. As it was, a rocket bomb exploded in a mortar pit, killing one, seriously wounding another and slightly wounding a third. The defenders had hardly got into position when the fanatical Javanese infantry attacked, penetrating the perimeter wire and capturing the mortar position whose crew had been hit in the opening bombardment.

Cpl Baughan, the acting platoon sergeant, had his shelter destroyed by a rocket bomb in the first burst of fire. Although stunned by the blast, he immediately checked to see that the other men were uninjured, then sent them to their stand-to posts. In spite of the fierce bombardment, he then made his way to a machine-gun post where he took command, steadied the young soldiers and brought their defensive fire under control, sweeping the ridge from which the rockets were being launched.

CSM Williams was in overall command, controlling the defensive fire, and quickly formed a section counter-attack to retake the mortar post. Cpl Baughan led this, and a sharp fight developed at very short range. Three Paras were wounded, and the section pinned down. Williams ran across the open ground under heavy fire to man a machine-gun post from which he could fire into the mortar pit. This enabled Baughan and his men to charge into the pit and dispatch the Javanese. So within ten minutes of its capture, the mortar pit had been retaken.

At about 0545 a second assault developed across the wire to the south of the perimeter. Nearly a score of enemy troops pressed to within a few feet of the trenches directly opposite Williams's position. One Javanese, wounded in the leg at the bottom of the hill, stopped to apply a rough tourniquet before continuing to advance with his heavy rocket-launcher. This illustrates the toughness of these troops whose fanatical attacks were on a par with those of the Japanese in Burma. Heavy fire from automatics and rocket-launchers at point-blank range rocked the Para positions. Williams was hit by splinters and blinded in one eye. The radio set by his side was struck, and the weapon he was using at the time received direct hits on two occasions, but the Paras held fast.

At about 0630 the Javanese were seen withdrawing towards the south-west. A follow-up was mounted at once by the other Para companies. Several platoons were roped down by helicopter behind the enemy hoping to ambush the escape routes, while a company of the 1/6th Gurkhas followed up the withdrawal routes on foot. The Indonesians' route was marked by large blood trails, many bloodstained dressings, and abandoned equipment. Long columns carrying dead and wounded were seen by villagers in surrounding kampongs. The signs indicated that the raiders had about thirty casualties. Only two bodies, however, were recovered.

Following the attack on Plaman Mapu, the Indonesians continued to show a close interest in the area. There were indications of a further and more powerful attack being planned using heavier supporting fire which necessitated the dumping of reserve ammunition in the jungle.

Reports came in from Mongkus of small enemy reconnaissance parties in the area. At 0710 on 15 May, villagers from a kampong to which a line had been laid to enable the Border Scouts to communicate quickly with D Company, telephoned to say that seventy Indonesians had been seen in the kampong the previous night. Major Barnes, the OC, at once sent out 10 Platoon. He strongly suspected an induced ambush, and the follow-up was conducted very gingerly. After a few hundred yards the tracks divided into three. Avoiding an obvious ambush area, the Paras contoured around a hill and entered an Indonesian ambush from a flank.

The ambush, manned by about a hundred men, had been cleverly prepared overlooking the obvious approaches along the track and stream bed. But the unexpected direction of the Paras' approach, forced the enemy to spring the ambush blind, and at this moment the majority of the patrol was defiladed by a slope. One man was killed but most of the fire went over their heads. Outnumbered three to one, the British troops, nevertheless, charged immediately, firing controlled and well-aimed shots at close range which accounted for five Indonesians. As the Red Berets stormed in, the enemy broke and fled. Five separate blood patches were found but as usual the Indonesians got their casualties away. Artillery fire was called down on the withdrawal routes and later large blood trails were discovered in several places.

The follow-up continued after dark, the Iban tracker using his hands literally to feel out the route until the smell of the enemy became overpowering. It was 0200 when the patrol halted, very close to the enemy.

At first light the Para force gained the border ridge and found another post for over a hundred men which had been vacated only about twenty minutes earlier. More artillery fire was called down, and the follow-up continued along the border ridge. Three entry and exit tracks were found for a total of two hundred men.

On 22 May locals reported tracks of a hundred men between

Mongkus and Mujat. Fifty had returned to the border, and the remainder had moved south into the same area where the previous ambushes had been set. The Security Forces put in an immediate helicopter assault. Seven platoons of 2 Para were roped down into the newly-constructed roping areas on the border ridge. The artillery had first fired suppression, and then armed helicopters had attacked each area, before the troop-carrying helicopters arrived. After 10 Platoon had been roped down, Cpl Tindale was sent with his section to search the border ridge. A short distance along the ridge he heard movement in the trees ahead and at once put his section into ambush. Abruptly, some forty Indonesians broke cover and advanced across the fairly open spine of the ridge.

The Para section held its fire until the enemy was about six yards away, then the two Bren guns mowed down at least fourteen Indonesians. This proved to be an advance party, and the following troops counter-attacked around the flank. When enemy mortar bombs hit the ridge on which the section lay, Tindale decided that the situation was too hot for comfort and withdrew without suffering any casualties.

The Parachute Battalion stayed in Borneo until 8 July when it was relieved, moved to Singapore, and then flown back to the United Kingdom. During its short stay the battalion had come up against a crack Javanese battalion which had shown enterprise, aggressiveness, and a high standard of battle discipline. But 2 Para had had the better of the exchange. Three British soldiers were killed and eight wounded. The Indonesians' casualties were at least thirty-eight killed, although the actual total must have been a good deal higher.

TWENTY
The Commonwealth Brigade

For some time the Commonwealth Brigade had been stationed in West Malaysia. Early in 1965 it was decided to move the 3rd Battalion Royal Australian Regiment, and the 1st Battalion Royal New Zealand Infantry Regiment, to Borneo. The 3rd RAR was put into the First Division, taking over from the 1/7th Gurkhas. The change over went smoothly and Gurkha and Australian made the most of the traditional hand-over parties.

Towards the end of May, Lt Patrick Beale was ordered to ambush a river which, according to an unconfirmed report, the Indonesians were using as a supply route. After leading his platoon through difficult and poorly mapped country, Beale left the bulk of his men in a defensive position near the river, while he continued with a reconnaissance party of three men to select the best ambush site. Six tense hours followed because they had to avoid enemy parties heard in the area, and the delay prevented the laying of the ambush that day. The following morning Beale settled into an ambush position along the river line with twelve of his men.

On the right flank was Pte Jackson, from Co Durham, who had joined the Australian Army. It was Jackson who first sighted a large party of Indonesians approaching in two boats. He cautiously alerted the ambush.

The chug-chug of the outboard motors seemed very loud as the Australians waited silently behind their weapons. But before the ambush was triggered, Jackson saw two more boats in the distance. He was unable to attract Beale's attention, and in that moment the lieutenant gave the order to open fire. The automatic weapons raked the two leading boats, killing the occupants. Jackson, finding that he was the only one who could see the other boats, took them on himself. Rapid and accurate rifle fire accounted for all five Indonesians in the third boat, but the fourth pulled quickly out of sight to the near bank. Jackson hurled grenades in the direction of the boat, then, regardless of Indonesian small arms fire from near and far banks, he climbed to a higher position from which he could effectively engage the occupants of the last boat with rifle fire. Beale now ordered the withdrawal of the ambush party, and they slipped away without loss in spite of the heavy volume of enemy fire. The Australian platoon had killed at least fifteen Indonesians.

The 3rd RAR continued to dominate the Bau District. On 12 June, 2/Lt Byers moved into an ambush site on a track recently used by the Indonesians. He had orders to remain in position for at least four days.

By the afternoon of the 15th the platoon had drawn a blank, and just when it seemed that the long vigil had been a waste of time a large party of Indonesians was heard approaching along the track. Byers waited until some twenty-five of the enemy had entered the killing ground before he triggered the ambush. Small arms fire swept across the track killing at least seventeen Indonesians and wounding the remainder. The main enemy party retaliated at once and two Australians were wounded. A fierce battle raged for ten minutes, with Byers calling on the artillery for DF fire which came down immediately and accurately, causing the enemy to move back in confusion. Taking advantage of this, Byers skilfully extricated his force from the danger area: he moved to a landing pad and the wounded were evacuated by helicopter.

On 30 June 1965 a platoon of the 1st Royal New Zealand Infantry Regiment moved up Track 53 from Lubok Antu in the Second Division to a position some six hundred yards short of the border. The platoon commander, Lt Marshall, had orders to ambush the general area of Track 63 and Track 63A. He was accompanied by Capt Harbans Singh and four members of 1 Malaysian Artillery. Reaching the waiting area shortly before midday, Marshall positioned his platoon into all-round defence with a Bren placed fifty yards up each track as sentry weapons. He then moved forward with a reconnaissance party, to look for a likely ambush area near the junction of Tracks 63 and 63A.

At 1220 one of the Bren gun sentries, Pte Ashby, saw three

162

Indonesians approaching the platoon's firm base. He immediately alerted the platoon which stood to in readiness. The leading enemy was twenty yards away when the man behind him saw one of the New Zealanders. Realizing this, Ashby shot the second man, and then turned his Bren on to the first man who was by then returning fire. Both the Indonesians were severely wounded and captured; the third disappeared among the scrub.

The front New Zealand section immediately cleared the area to within one hundred and fifty yards of the platoon position, while Capt Harbans Singh brought down artillery fire onto the border and the edge of the jungle to block all routes out of the area. Nothing more could be done at this stage because the reconnaissance group was somewhere between the platoon and the border.

When Marshall heard the firing he moved to within twenty-five yards of the track junction and spotted a group of Indonesians preparing a mortar for firing. The reconnaisance group at once opened fire. Two of the mortar crew were seriously hit, and it seemed almost certain that a third had also been wounded. The remainder of the mortar crew gave covering fire while their wounded were dragged out of sight.

Marshall was very anxious to rejoin his command, and so he moved his group back to the firm base. With their return artillery fire could be brought down close to the enemy position.

The second captured Indonesian was very badly wounded, but before he died he said that he was part of a forward group of fifteen, and that a larger party of soldiers was following some distance behind. Marshall promptly asked Harbans Singh to seal off the approach of this larger group. With the Malaysian gunners building a wall of artillery shells, Marshall moved forward again to search the area. He led two sections along Track 63 until he reached the point where the mortar crew had been engaged earlier. Hiding in low scrub twenty yards to the west were two Indonesians. One was wounded but the other was very active and hurled a grenade, following up with a long burst from his Madsen sub-machine gun. The grenade failed to explode and the bullets were wide of their target. The New Zealanders killed them both.

Marshall cleared the remainder of Track 63 as far as the border, swung east to search the jungle fringe, then back along

63A to the firm base. It was now obvious that his action had forestalled an attempted incursion by some seventy Indonesians into Lubok Antu.

At five o'clock that evening, the lieutenant's company commander ordered him forward to the initial contact area in order to ambush the junction of the tracks. With only half an hour of light left, the platoon moved quickly into position. Two Claymore mines were placed, but weapon pits could not be dug because of the noise and the lack of time.

Placing sentries, Marshall stood the platoon down. Apart from the usual jungle noises, the night was quiet until an hour after midnight when an unexplained noise was heard to the south-east. At once the platoon stood to. Ten minutes later a large group of Indonesians opened fire from a range of one hundred yards. Machine-gun and rifle bullets whined overhead for about five minutes, then the enemy moved back another hundred yards. At this a 60 mm mortar boomed out, the bombs falling initially to the west and then within seventy-five yards of the New Zealanders. Marshall at once called down the DF artillery tasks previously registered by the FOO. Because of the accuracy of the enemy fire, both from mortar and small arms, Marshall thought that his location had been pin-pointed. As his position also prohibited the use of closer artillery DFs, he decided to move five hundred yards to the north and take up a further fighting ambush site. In deep darkness the platoon packed the remainder of its gear and moved to a rendezvous on Track 63 where they were checked to see that all were present. By now the Malaysian gunners had effectively silenced the enemy mortar, and there was a ten minute lull in the firing.

Marshall was about to move out when he heard a noise in the area of the Claymore mines previously laid down. He fired these before withdrawing north to the new ambush site. The artillery shelled the area west and east of the track to stop the enemy moving forward while the platoon was reorganizing. Despite this it was a difficult move, with no moon or starlight. A hundred yard length of guide string was used with each man attached to it. Marshall led this silent column into the new ambush position by 0230. Five minutes later the Indonesians fired again on the old site with a 2-inch mortar and small arms. Marshall then realized that the enemy was unaware of the exact location of his old site and knew nothing of his move to the new position. The mortar flashes were seen by the 1 RNZIR Recce Platoon commander in an OP to the west, and he brought down further artillery fire. The enemy then ceased fire and withdrew.

Several of the New Zealand Regiment personnel were seconded to the SAS. One of these was Lt Eru Ihaka Manuera. On 19 April 1965 he led a four man SAS patrol to locate an enemy camp in Sarawak. This he did most successfully, approaching to within fifty yards of the camp, and keeping it under observation for six hours. The patrol then returned to base with valuable information about the location and layout of the camp, enemy strength, and equipment.

On 16 May Manuera returned with his patrol to ambush the camp. Approaching the area in darkness, they were in position fifty yards from the camp before first light. The ambush site covered the line of a river which ran alongside the camp; and shortly after daybreak Manuera saw four Indonesians enter a longboat and move upstream towards his position. Silently the patrol waited until the longboat was opposite their position and then raked it from stem to stern. Manuera killed one soldier, while the rest of his patrol killed two more, and wounded the fourth. Another Indonesian had selected this moment to take a bath near the far bank, and he was also dispatched.

With the enemy camp aroused, the SAS withdrew. But the Indonesians, showing considerable initiative, had sent a section to set up a quick ambush on the patrol's escape route. The idea was good but the shooting was atrocious, and they missed at very short range. Manuera, after a quick blaze of fire at the enemy, moved his patrol to high ground. He then returned to a point from where he could observe the enemy. The Indonesian section leader was attempting to rally his men; Manuera promptly shot and seriously wounded him. While the enemy was in a state of leaderless confusion, he was able to direct the fire of his patrol amongst them, killing two more. At this the remainder withdrew, and the SAS patrol returned to base safely.

TWENTY-ONE

Rivers and a Knife-edged Ridge

While the border war continued, the Security Forces in the second line of defence still had to contend with the CCO threat. For some time there had been no major aggressive operations by the CCO in Sarawak, and perhaps it was this which encouraged the District Officer of Serian, in the First Division, to consider that 'his people were all right'. He would not allow the detached troops of the 4 RTR to mount the extensive 'Hearts and Minds' and anti-CCO operations which were working so well in both the Bau and Kuching districts.

On 26 June 1965 Indonesia switched to outright terrorism against civilians on the pattern of the Malayan Emergency, taking advantage of the vacuum left in the Security Force defences in Serian. Two co-ordinated night raids were launched by a raiding party consisting of Indonesian regulars and volunteers who had slipped into the area to join up with local CCO which provided the arms and led the raids.

One attack went in on the 18th Milestone Police Station on the Semengo–Serian road. A policeman was shot and another fatally wounded. The terrorists then explored the neighbouring buildings and discovered a further policeman who was fatally wounded. To round off the attack they brutally murdered some innocent children who had come out of the buildings to see what all the firing was about.

A further raid was made on two Chinese families. Altogether eight civilians, including the policemen, were killed in the two raids. The brutality, including the hanging of a number of Chinese, within ten miles of Kuching threw the local loyal Chinese into abject terror, which, of course, was the CCO's intention—to terrorize into submission.

Earlier, a routine convoy had set off from Semengo for Serian, escorted by Sergeant Brown of C Squadron in the leading

4 RTR armoured car, and some five miles of convoy behind him with L/Cpl Bellamy-Brown as 'tail-end Charlie'. On the look out for trouble, Sergeant Brown suddenly saw five large wooden blocks in the middle of the road with six-inch nails protruding from them. Scattered around the blocks were patches of oil. He gingerly removed the blocks to the side of the road, and the convoy continued. Minutes later the skyline ahead flashed red and the roar of an explosion rolled back. The sergeant told his driver to speed up and the armoured car accelerated to the 24th milestone. There he found the bridge partly collapsed with smoke still rising from the sagging beams. Brown made a brief search and discovered two of the saboteurs lying dead under it. The charge had been placed in an amateurish way, and the bridge was still crossable.

The convoy arrived soon afterwards at Serian and found a general alert in progress. It was then Brown realized that his convoy must have passed the 18th milestone just before or just after the raid on the Police Station.

Security Forces rushed to the scene and arrived at the 18th Milestone Police Station around midnight. It was obvious that because of the absence of patrols, road blocks, and searches the CCO's campaign of fear and intimidation had found fertile soil to work upon. It proved that no matter what local administrators might feel, there could be no let up in anti-CCO activities. When it was already too late, patrols and road blocks were once again instituted.

Following the attack on the 18th Milestone Police Station, a decision was made to launch Operation Hammer—the screening and resettling of all the local Chinese. Some eight thousand Chinese were evacuated from the border area to a new resettlement area about fifteen miles from Kuching on the Serian Road. Without the endless escorting, patrolling, and radio communications provided by the Sarawak Squadron (4 RTR), the task would have been much more difficult. Moving so many people, along with their belongings, their pigs and their ducks, was a major operation. It was carried out in two separate phases each lasting a week. Although the actual moving of these people was undertaken by the civil authorities, the Security Forces were involved. The 1/7th Gurkhas found them 'incredibly friendly and cheerful, both adults and children—so unlike the sullen

167

morose and unco-operative resettled Chinese in Malaya during the Emergency.'

It was this cheerfulness and friendliness which decided Lt-Col Carroll, commanding the 1/7th, to launch Operation Tiger Balm. The force consisted of the battalion's Pipes and Drums, HQ basketball team, and an elite selection of spectators from Battalion HQ. When a further party of some 350 Chinese had moved into their permanent houses in the resettlement following Operation Tea Cup just before Christmas, the Tiger Balm team sallied forth. Every evening for a month the Pipes and Drums played in various kampongs and longhouses, while the remainder distributed peanuts and lollipops to the children. By the time the 1/7th left Sarawak early in 1966 they had been to nearly every kampong and longhouse in the Battalion area and made friends in them all.

In August 1965 the 2/2nd Gurkha Rifles moved to Lundu in the First Division. The countryside was very flat, intersected by large, meandering rivers, with occasional Gunongs or rocky limestone outcrops, and matted with primary and secondary jungle. When it rained the whole countryside could be turned into a swamp of uncertain depth in a matter of hours, a combination that made patrolling physically difficult and unpleasant. The border with Indonesia was only a line drawn on the map; there was no physical line of demarcation on the ground. The Indonesians were quick to take advantage of this fact, as any incursion could be explained away by 'bad map-reading' or self-adjusting boundary lines.

But the nature of Lundu was also to the Gurkhas' advantage; for the rivers, winding their tortuous routes across the flat, jungle-covered plain, often cut the border as marked on the map and so presented ambush targets in the shape of Indonesian boat patrols actually inside the battalion's area. Lt-Col Neill was not slow to make the most of this bonus.

The Support Company, temporarily under command of Capt (QGO) Surendraman Gurung, opened the battalion's score, which was to rise to mercurial heights by the end of its tour. On 1 August Surendraman established a firm patrol base, then carried out an extensive reconnaissance to pick the best ambush site on a river bank in the area. The following morning he led his men to the ambush site. Although he expected the enemy to use the river, he also covered the land side; an hour later eight armed Indonesian soldiers approached along the track which followed the river bank. As they neared the far end of the ambush fire was opened and all the soldiers were killed.

Towards the end of August, Neill ordered the Support Company, commanded by Major Christopher Bullock, and elements from A and C Companies, to lay ambushes along a river. Steady rain had turned the ground for thousands of yards from the river banks into swamps which were shoulder-deep or even deeper. The Gurkhas pressed on in appalling conditions to try and find ambush sites at the river's edge, but so much of the countryside was waterlogged that it was difficult to distinguish the river from the land.

A and C Companies approached their objectives first. Major Ashley of C Company established a base, then waded and swam forward with his ambush party to try and find the river, but it was indistinguishable in the watery maze.

Major Lauderdale of A Company was in similar straits, and Neill, after close examination of air photographs, suggested an alternative route. The move from the patrol bases involved a wide detour which needed courage and resourcefulness to negotiate. At one stage temporary bridges had to be built to get across particularly treacherous sectors, but eventually the river was reached.

A boat was seen that evening but did not constitute a target. The next day another boat, moving slowly upriver against the current, entered the ambush sector manned by the A Company element. Fire was opened on the ten Indonesians who attempted to return the fire. But the Gurkhas' crossfire was too fierce and accurate, and all ten were quickly dispatched. A and C Companies then withdrew through their firm bases to the nearest helicopter LZ, and returned by air to their company sites.

Meanwhile the Support Company had also tried to move into a separate river ambush. Bullock carried out a reconnaissance in swamp ranging from waist to neck deep. Soaked to the skin, his arms aching from holding his SLR out of the water, his eyes smarting from the glare of the sun reflected on the flood water, Bullock must have despaired of ever finding the river. Then suddenly the slush beneath his feet gave way to firm ground, and he realized that by good fortune he had hit upon what must have been a logging track extending back from the river's edge. Heartened by this discovery, he led the way along the hidden path through shoulder-deep water. From time to time one of the Gurkhas would inadvertently step off the track and submerge in the deeper water. Pressing on, Bullock discovered two trees at the edge of the river where it was possible to set a seven-man ambush. This was rather less than the fifty to one hundred yard ambush he had intended to lay. Still, at least he had found the river.

For the rest of that day the ambush stayed in position, up to their necks in water. Early the next morning they were back on the site. The water was so cold that the Gurkhas had to be changed over every one and a half hours; Bullock, however, stood in the ambush, up to his neck in the cold water, for three days unrelieved!

At last, on the third day, an enemy boat appeared on the chocolate-coloured river. At ten yards' range, the Gurkhas killed all four of the occupants. Immediately from some one hundred yards downriver came a great volume of fire. Apparently at least one other boat-load of troops was in the vicinity and reacted very sharply. Bullets lashed the water near the Gurkhas' heads like hailstones. Bullock decided it was time to withdraw. Hampered by the flood water and the mud, the ambush party dragged its way through the swamp to the patrol base.

The battalion maintained its relentless pressure on the enemy. Towards the end of August, Major Ashley of C Company sited two ambushes. One was on the river line, the other on a near-by track. The Gurkhas were in position for only a few hours when a boat manned by six Indonesians came into sight. All six were killed and the boat sunk.

Shortly afterwards, some thirty to forty Indonesians ran up the track towards the sound of the shooting. When the first fifteen were in the killing ground, Sgt Lalsing Thapa sprang the ambush, and all were accounted for. The remainder at once re-deployed to a flank to try and roll up the ambush. But they ran straight into the cut-off group and six more were killed and several wounded. Ashley then gave the order for the whole of C Company to withdraw. The action had accounted for twenty-seven Indonesians. This brought the battalion's total kills to forty-nine in one month without loss. Only a few months later the total was to reach over one hundred and twenty—the highest any battalion had achieved in Borneo since the start of Confrontation.

On 2 September 1965, Bullock again went forward with his Support Company to lay a river ambush. Having found a suitable site, he placed his men along the river line, with the Recce Platoon on the right and the Assault Pioneer Platoon on the left. The centre was filled by WO II Deoparsad Gurung and the Anti-Tank Platoon, and Bullock with his HQ. To the rear, a check-point was manned by Capt Masters, the artillery FOO, and CSM Hariparsad Gurung together with a signaller and a medical orderly.

On the right flank the Recce Platoon Commander heard movement on the landward side to his right. The wooded bank was full of the enemy who, instead of using the river, had approached by land. The Recce Platoon cut down twelve of the enemy in a few minutes. Counter-fire swept along the bank. The weight of enemy fire increased rapidly, indicating the presence of a considerable force. Then the Indonesians tried to over-run the outnumbered Support Company by rolling the ambush from right to left. The Recce Platoon repulsed this attempt, so the enemy tried a rapid encircling movement.

By now Bullock had moved to the right flank to gauge the situation, and realized that his men were in danger of being cut off. He decided to withdraw, first pulling the Recce Platoon back through the Anti-Tank Platoon; but while this was being done, the Anti-Tank Platoon suddenly opened fire, which at first sight looked very risky as they seemed to be firing on their own men. Bullock heaved a sigh of relief when he realized that the target was an enemy force on the far bank who were firing rifle grenades across the river. The Anti-Tank Platoon's spirited reply soon silenced this attack, and the withdrawal continued.

Next, the Assault Pioneers pulled in from the left flank to hold the check-point, while the Anti-Tank Platoon withdrew. The battle was fast turning into a mêlée, and only outstanding leadership, marksmanship, and individual gallantry enabled the Gurkhas to make a clean break. They left behind many Indonesian dead and wounded.

But just when Bullock thought that all his men were clear, he found that the check-point party was missing. He immediately went back with Sgt Bhagtasing Gurung and L/Cpl Resembahadur Thapa. Moving stealthily through the undergrowth, they approached the ambush site and, crouching, called softly, hoping the party was still there. The undergrowth rustled, and the shapes of a large enemy force materialized out of the jungle background! Resembahadur thrust Bullock to one side, stood up, adjusted the carrying sling of his Bren gun over one shoulder, pushed his hat to the back of his head and gave the enemy two and a half magazines of rapid fire. The Indonesians went down like flies in the face of this one-man barrage, and it was impossible to estimate how many were killed or wounded.

Still, it was clearly not the time to drag one's feet, and the searchers hurriedly rejoined the company. A second check revealed that Capt Masters, Sgt Hariparsad, and the signaller were missing. But they had been seen to move off when the withdrawal was completed. Bullock reported the situation to his colonel on the radio, and was told to break with the enemy as quickly and cleanly as possible. This he did, and that night found the group in a suitable bivouac.

The following morning the ambush party moved to the nearest company base. The missing signaller had already arrived there. He had been separated from the other two, when virtually surrounded by the enemy, and had made his way back some ten thousand yards without map or compass. Then, still before the Support Company's arrival, an exhausted Capt Masters reached the same company base about 1630 with a story to tell.

During the river bank battle and the subsequent withdrawal, Masters and Hariparsad became separated from the rest of the force, and were suddenly surrounded by the enemy. A burst of fire wounded the Gurkha twice in the left leg, and at the same time Masters tripped and fell. Thinking that both were shot, the Indonesians started to close in. Masters at once opened fire, hitting two of the enemy.

It was a moment of grave danger. Masters crouched beside the wounded sergeant, comforting him, and standing guard. In the next moment, near-by members of the Support Company engaged the enemy and under this covering fire, Masters lifted Hariparsad and carried him along what he thought to be the

18. Royal Marine Commandos patrolling by assault craft on the Serudong in Sabah.

19. An Indonesian paratrooper is captured by the Gurkhas. Still wearing his American pattern combat suit he is blindfolded before being flown out for questioning.

20. Corporal Rambahadur Limbu, 10th Gurkha Rifles, who won the only Victoria Cross awarded during Confrontation. He was the thirteenth Gurkha to win the VC in the Brigade of Gurkhas' 150 years history.

withdrawal route. In the dense jungle he lost contact with the remainder of the company, and realized that he must make his own way back to base with the wounded Gurkha.

Hoisting Hariparsad on to his back, he set off through the jungle. With no hand free to cut a track, he had to force his way through the undergrowth. The sinewy branches sprang back as he pushed through, beating against his body. Unable to protect his face, he was lashed by sharp twigs till rivulets of blood ran down his cheeks and mingled with the beads of perspiration. Unseen creepers tripped him up, and he had to fall awkwardly to protect the Gurkha on his back. Each time the effort to get up again and to keep moving was more difficult. Somehow he kept his feet going. Then the hard ground gave way to swamp. In a moment he was up to his thighs in the black, oozing mud, each dragging movement forward followed by a squelching noise which stirred up the evil, rotting smell of the swamp. The hot afternoon sun beat down through the gaps in the tall trees, and the tracery of the jungle shimmered in the intense heat haze. The perspiration rolled down his forehead into his eyes, blurring his vision. His face burned with the heat. His body ached with the weight of the wounded Gurkha. There were few dry places to rest, and in any case he knew that to stop would probably be fatal. At times to ease the weight on his back, he lowered Hariparsad on to the mud and dragged him inch by inch, before he felt strong enough to hoist him on to his back again.

At last the shadows lengthened and darkness fell. The heat was still trapped in the overhang of the jungle, but the air seemed cooler, and at least the blinding glare had gone. Masters continued in the darkness until about 1930 when he decided to take a rest. He had carried or dragged Hariparsad through six thousand yards of dense jungle and swamp.

The next morning he awoke early, his body aching and stiff. With a great effort he hoisted Hariparsad on to his back and resumed the journey. But he had gone only a very short distance when he realized that he could move no further under the burden of the wounded man. Wisely he appreciated that there was a much better chance of saving both their lives if he continued alone to the nearest Security Force base and returned with help. He explained this to Hariparsad and left with him all the food he had and his second water bottle.

After a nightmare journey on a compass bearing through more thick jungle and swamp, Masters reached the company base in remarkable time by late that afternoon. Although exhausted, he insisted on accompanying the rescue party to find Hariparsad. It was no easy task to locate him and it was late the next day before he was found. By this time he had lost a lot of blood and gangrene had set in. Had his evacuation been postponed further he would undoubtedly have lost a leg. As it was, the story had a happy ending; the operation was a complete success, and Hariparsad was discharged from hospital without even a limp.

In August 1965 Lt-Col Myers' 2/10th Gurkha Rifles relieved the 3rd Royal Australian Regiment in the First Division. When A Company Commander, Major Lund, took over a forward sector from his Australian counterpart he was told, with great solemnity, that this included 'the finest loo in Sarawak'. The Australians had built a superb 'seven-holer', using vast quantities of cement. But Lund soon found that this sanitary wonder harboured too great a number of flies for his comfort and ordered a smoke grenade to be dropped inside in an attempt to get rid of the flies. Unfortunately, a white phosphorus grenade was used by accident, and 'the whole edifice went majestically up and outwards'.

When the battalion had completed the take-over, the new British light-weight ration was tried out to see if the Gurkhas would take to it, or at least be prepared to eat it, on a long ten-to-fourteen-day patrol. One evening, when a platoon made camp, as time was short, the men decided to eat their ration cold. One newly-joined rifleman emptied a packet of egg-powder direct into his mouth, and soon found his jaws welded together and his teeth surrounded by an immovable yellow mass. His frantic actions to free his teeth, and the frothing around his mouth, led his companions to believe that he had either seen a *bhut* (devil) or was suffering a maniacal fit. Finally someone sat on his chest, prised open his jaws and discovered the real reason.

Another pair of Gurkhas, coming off sentry duty in the early hours of the morning, felt rather peckish. In the dark they chose a tit-bit at random out of the ration pack and, having taken off the outer cover, broke it in two and ate it. In the morning they found that they had consumed a book of matches.

When the battalion moved to Borneo Myers had looked forward to numerous fierce encounters with the Indonesians. The build-up of enemy forces and the now almost exclusive use of regulars had brought the size and scope of the actions far from the skirmishes with volunteers of the early days. But he hardly expected that one battle would bring to the 2/10th Gurkhas world-wide fame.

In November 1965, information was received that the Indonesians were establishing a guerrilla base in the Bau District. At once Capt Maunsell, C Company Commander, was sent with a strong force to locate the position and destroy it. The country was very difficult, with knife-edged ridges enmeshed in thick secondary jungle, leading to hilltops covered in primary jungle. Nearing the area on the afternoon of the first day, Maunsell sent Lt (QGO) Ranjit Rai, commanding 7 Platoon, on a reconnaissance. He scoured the range until he caught sight of the Indonesian position and then returned to report to Maunsell.

The captain's problem was to find the best approach route for his attack. The following morning he made a personal reconnaissance with his 8 Platoon Commander, Lt (QGO) Bhagat Bahadur Rai, and also dispatched Lt (QGO) Puransing Limbu of 9 Platoon to reconnoitre the area from an alternative direction.

Unobserved by the enemy, Maunsell made a careful study of their position. On one of the hilltops a platoon base was being constructed. It was a formidable position, for the hill had sheer sides and three approaches along steep, narrow ridges. Two of the ridges and the deep valleys were covered in dense secondary jungle, giving the position almost the same protection as an apron of barbed wire. Five hundred yards down the west ridge was the usual enemy counter-attack force of at least company strength.

The base was still in the process of construction, but already more than two-thirds complete, and Maunsell could see the fatigue parties still at work. He turned his attention from them to the two possible approach routes, and after careful thought chose the south ridge.

175

At 0600 on the third morning, he set off with his force, and by 0830 had reached the point from where Ranjit had made his reconnaissance on the first day. Here, eight hundred yards from the south ridge, the men ate a meal. When they moved off about half an hour later, the Pioneer Platoon, under Sgt Dhankarna Rai, was left to form a rear base with the FOO. Maunsell continued through the jungle for another four hundred yards at right angles to the ridge, until he reached an almost impenetrable tangle of secondary jungle. Here he left Sgt-Major Indrahang Limbu and a section from 9 Platoon to guard the RV point.

There then began the long, tough task of cutting a tunnel through the jungle. Silently and stealthily, Maunsell and three Gurkhas cut a four hundred yard tunnel, using the battalion's secret weapon—secateurs! It was slow, hot work, at the rate of one hundred yards an hour; but the steady clip of the pruners gradually brought them nearer to the ridge. By 1330 the leading group had reached the lower slope. Two scouts crouched ahead. Behind was Maunsell with his platoon commanders. They could see the enemy base about sixty feet above, but in between were further obstacles. The Indonesians had cut down trees to block the five-foot wide ridge. The Gurkhas were about to clear the first of these barriers, when they heard the rustle of leaves a few yards beyond. There was a tense twenty minutes while they waited in complete silence, not moving a muscle. A man was obviously working on a second barrier. Then they heard him moving away, and he came into view near the top of the hill.

The man obviously suspected nothing, and as soon as he was out of sight, the Gurkhas cleared the barrier, came up to the second one which the man had been working on and cut their way through this as well. At that moment another Indonesian appeared at the top of the hill. He must have seen some movement, for he began to unsling his rifle, and had to be shot. Surprise was now lost and the assault was launched at once.

Ranjit's platoon moved to the left and 8 Platoon to the right in single file. Straight up the ridge stood a hut. If there was a machine gun there it could sweep the ridge. Speed was essential. Four abreast, the Gurkhas charged up the ridge, a sheer drop on either side. A machine gun opened up from the left, and a bullet knicked the arm of a Gurkha. There was a momentary

176

pause. Ranjit realized that any check in momentum at this crucial stage could not only affect the morale of those with him in the lead, but also result in greater losses to those still confined to the narrow ridge behind him. Rushing forward with four of his men, he hurled several hand grenades which stopped the fire for a few vital seconds. He stormed the hut, killed the occupants and thus took the first objective.

Maunsell, moving with the leading men, passed through the hut to take up his control point just beyond, from where he could conduct the battle. He ordered Bhagat to attack from the right and clear the ground to the next line of enemy fortifications. By this time the Indonesians had rushed to man the trenches and a heavy hail of fire met the attacking Gurkhas who immediately went to ground. One Gurkha rose to his feet and charged, firing from the hip, but he received the full burst of a machine gun and was killed instantly. Another Gurkha was seriously wounded. Maunsell ordered covering fire while he crawled forward and pulled the wounded man back behind the crest. This individual act of extreme gallantry was seen by many of his men and the effect was immediate. Bhagat led a concentrated rush and the men followed up, hurling grenades and firing from the hip, to take the enemy trenches.

On the other flank, after Ranjit had stormed the hut, L/Cpl Rambahadur Limbu swung to the left with his Bren gunner and the number two in order to silence a troublesome enemy machine gun. This was only Rambahadur's second time in action, but with complete disregard for his safety he led his cover group across the fire-swept ground. Charging through the open jungle, he spotted the first enemy machine gunner in a trench and killed him with a hand grenade. By this time at least two more machine guns were sweeping the area, and the corporal and his men took cover in the trench. Rambahadur realized that the machine guns had to be knocked out. Ignoring the hail of bullets, he left the safety of his trench and moved with his fire group to a big tree near by. On the way they passed another trench. At once, the number one dropped a grenade into it, and dived to the ground. A hand grasping an automatic appeared above the lip of the trench to fire an unaimed burst which hit the numbers one and two. A split second later, the grenade detonated and killed the Indonesian.

177

With his fire group out of action, Rambahadur tried to contact his platoon commander to advise him of the position, but he was unable to make himself heard over the noise of the battle and at the same time Ranjit was busy clearing another trench. Rambahadur started to crawl towards the hut, and machine-gun bullets whined dangerously close. He decided that he would have to bring his men to safety himself, as he was sure they were still alive. He crawled forward again, and the enemy fire seemed to increase as bullets cut the ground around him. He turned to crawl back towards the hut but checked himself before reaching it. He could not leave his men near the big tree, exposed to more fire. He decided that speed alone could give him the cover the ground could not afford, and springing to his feet he ran forward. Picking up the first man, he carried him to the hut. Then, without hesitation, he immediately returned and carried the other man back through a hail of bullets.

'That he was able to achieve what he did without being hit was miraculous,' said his commanding officer. 'His outstanding personal bravery, selfless conduct, complete contempt of the enemy and his determination to save the lives of the men of his fire group set an incomparable example and inspired all who saw him.' It had taken him twenty minutes to bring back the two men. Unfortunately, in spite of his great effort, it was found that both the Gurkhas were dead.

Although Rambahadur had risked his life twice in crossing the gap between the hut and the tree, he now made a third run, this time to collect the Bren gun lying by the trench. A few men from his platoon followed because Ranjit wanted the machine guns on the left destroyed. Passing unharmed through the hail of bullets, Rambahadur picked up the Bren, and launched an attack on the distant Indonesian machine guns. He charged through the open jungle, Bren gun blazing from the hip, inspiring his comrades, and putting the enemy guns out of action. Rambahadur personally killed at least four Indonesians.

Now only the rear position remained to be taken. Ranjit brought up his platoon and moving round the area already secured by Bhagat's platoon, he led the final and successful flanking charge which destroyed the last of the enemy. With the entire position now in his hands, Maunsell expected a counter-attack to come in at any moment. But it arrived from an unexpected quarter. Firing broke out from beyond the tunnel in the direction of 9 Platoon. The Gurkhas could not see the enemy, just the smoke from their weapons. Cpl Krishnabahadur Rai fired a one-hundred-and-fifty-round burst from his GPMG into the jungle. The enemy ceased firing and the counter-attack faded away.

Now Lt (QGO) Bhuwansing Limbu spread his Recce Platoon along the approach ridge, together with the remainder of 9 Platoon, in anticipation of further attacks. Almost at once, two Indonesian soldiers appeared on the south-west ridge running almost parallel to the approach ridge. The Gurkha ridge burst into fire, like a broadside from a ship; every weapon went off at the same time, and the two enemy soldiers virtually disintegrated. A few moments later, three more Indonesians were seen in almost the same spot and received the same treatment. At this, the Indonesians started firing mortars at the Recce and 9 Platoons, the bombs exploding within ten yards. The Gurkhas retaliated with 2-inch mortars, and must have been on target, because the enemy mortars ceased firing.

After these spasmodic attempts to counter-attack, the Indonesians put in a more concerted effort. Six men, using fire and movement, started to attack along the parallel ridge. This meant three going forward covered by the other three. Then the latter would pass through to the next bound, and so on in stages. This is a fine theory of fieldcraft but as three of the Indonesians rose to their feet on the run forward, there was another broadside from the Gurkha ridge, and they were all killed.

Now the most dangerous enemy movement began. The Indonesian reinforcements moved up, over seventy strong, along the third ridge in a fierce counter-attack. As they approached, Maunsell radioed the FOO and asked for ten rounds artillery fire. The gunners obliged very quickly, but the first shells to scream over the top of the jungle exploded almost amongst the Gurkhas. A large chunk of shrapnel carved a slice out of a tree only a few feet above Maunsell's head. He speedily called up the FOO again and altered the range. The next salvo lifted and was on target.

Maunsell decided that it was now time to move out. He had achieved his objectives; the enemy position had been destroyed and at least twenty-four Indonesians had been killed, probably many more. But the withdrawal was not going to be easy. There were three dead Gurkhas and one seriously wounded to be carried. A fourth Gurkha was only slightly wounded and could walk out.

In the thick jungle, it would need forty-eight men to evacuate the dead and wounded, twelve men per stretcher, carrying in groups of four for about ten minutes—the maximum in this terrible going. Men were detailed accordingly and Maunsell decided to make a straight exit from the right of the position to join the tunnel at right angles. The withdrawal was carried out in a clockwise movement. First, 8 Platoon, on the extreme right, set out down into the valley. They were followed by 7 Platoon, the Recce Platoon, and finally by 9 Platoon bringing up the rear, so that at all times the withdrawal was fully covered against counter-attacks. As soon as his men were clear, Maunsell ordered down a barrage of 5.5s and 105s on to the vacated position. The battle was over. It had lasted for about ninety minutes.

Capt Maunsell and Lt Ranjit Rai both received the MC, and Rambahadur Limbu was awarded the VC. His citation stated that he had 'displayed heroism, self-sacrifice and a devotion to duty and to his men of the very highest order. His actions on this day reached a zenith of determined, premeditated valour which must count among the most notable on record.' It was the thirteenth such award to be won by a Gurkha, and the first by a soldier of the 10th Princess Mary's Own Gurkha Rifles. Twenty-one years had passed since a Gurkha had last been awarded the VC. By a strange coincidence, on that occasion in 1945, when Lachhiman Gurung won the VC in Burma, his Company Commander was a young major named Peter Myers. That same officer, now a lieutenant-colonel, commanded Rambahadur's battalion.

TWENTY-TWO
A Rift and a Rebellion

The news on Monday, 9 August 1965, that Singapore had been ejected from Malaysia took officials and the public by surprise. The Malaysian High Commission in Belgrave Square first learned of the expulsion on reading a telegram from Kuala Lumpur when the office opened at 1000 on Monday. The Malaysian High Commissioner was on holiday in Norway. The announcement stated that as the result of many differences of opinion between the Central and Singapore Governments, it had been agreed that Singapore should secede from the Federation of Malaysia. The secession agreement had been signed on Saturday, 7 August, but for security reasons was not made public until two days later.

Tunku Abdul Rahman had made his decision to divorce Singapore while he was convalescing in London after an illness contracted during the Commonwealth Prime Ministers' Conference. The Deputy Prime Minister, Tun Abdul Razak, had discussed the problem for three weeks with a few select Malaysian Cabinet Ministers and Dr Goh Keng Swee, then Singapore's Minister of Finance. On 23 July Razak advised the Tunku that his senior colleagues agreed that Singapore must go. Within two days instructions for drafting the separation agreement and constitution amending bill had been given and Parliament was ordered to convene on 9 August. Singapore's Prime Minister, Lee Kuan Yew, waited until the Tunku returned, hoping to make him change his mind—but in vain.

What had caused the separation, and why did this great multi-racial experiment fail?

For some time there had been a duel of personalities between the aristocratic Malay Prime Minister and the brilliant, tough, Cambridge-educated, Chinese Prime Minister of Singapore. Lee Kuan Yew was widely regarded as the most formidable

181

politician in South-east Asia. A 'man in a hurry', he had been quietly contemptuous of the Tunku's lack of drive; the Tunku had, perhaps, envied Lee's reputation. Both men believed passionately in the Federation. Lee crusaded by means of the socialist People's Action Party for a multi-racial 'Malaysian Malaysia'. Critics of the Tunku accused him and his Alliance Party of favouring a 'Malayan Malaysia', giving preferential treatment to the Federation's indigenous Malays.

The more easy-going Malays were finding it increasingly difficult to compete with the bustling, energetic dedication of the commercially-minded Chinese, and they came to feel that they were fast becoming 'second-class citizens' in their own country.

Informed observers believed that the Tunku had accepted Singapore into Malaysia to prevent the risk of having a Communist neighbour on his doorstep. The Chinese had become extremely politically conscious and, under Lee's leadership, introduced PAP candidates on the mainland in the non-Malay areas. Lee also ran non-Chinese PAP candidates in the Malay constituences in the local elections in Singapore itself. In May 1965 he formed the Malaysian People's Solidarity Convention out of the various groups in the Federal Parliament. This was regarded by the Tunku as interference in Malaya's internal affairs.

From Lee's point of view, the absorption of Singapore into Malaysia had drastically affected his own status. Before the merger he had been the undisputed leader of a separate state; afterwards his status had declined. His action in running candidates against the Malayan Chinese Association failed owing to the Tunku's loyalty to those Chinese who had supported the Alliance. A dangerous situation arose when the stream of abuse from Singapore failed to divide the Chinese on the mainland and instead led to what was virtually an attack by the Chinese of Singapore on the Malays of Malaya. Tension increased daily and it was obvious that communal violence of unprecedented gravity was impending.

In a speech to the House of Representatives on 9 August 1965 the Tunku said that the Singapore State Government had ceased to give even a modicum of loyalty to the Central Government. Two measures were open to him: either to take repressive action against the leaders of the Singapore State Government,

182

or to sever all connection. The first step was repulsive to his conception of Parliamentary Democracy, and in any case would not solve the communal issue. 'I shall not be the instrument which causes my people to do internecine battle,' he said.

The Singapore leaders seemed to accept, albeit unwillingly, the view that the alternative to secession was bloodshed. Lee said that a long debate over the question might easily lead to reciprocal rioting and massacre. Once the leaders were convinced that the break was inevitable they saw no point in consulting the British Government who would only have counselled patience and compromise! If Tunku Abdul Rahman had wanted to fight off his extremists, they could have combined and saved the situation. 'But Tunku wanted his Malay rule *in toto*, and once he decided not to fight for us, the whole thing blows,' said Lee.

The news was undoubtedly grave for the whole of South-east Asia. Not only was the war in Vietnam hotting up, but now the amputation of Singapore seemed likely to weaken Malaysia's fight against Sukarno. The great tragedy was that Malaysia, the bright hope of democracy in Asia, had apparently come to grief mainly because the easy-going Malays envied the industrious Chinese settlers. Malaysia had been founded, two years previously, to overcome this very incompatibility. In Malaya the Malays had seen the Chinese settlers establish themselves as the core of the commercial community. In Singapore, the Chinese were overwhelmingly dominant. It was with difficulty that the Malays had managed to retain control of their country on gaining independence.

The moment of parting brought deep emotions to the surface. At a Press Conference in Singapore Lee Kuan Yew spoke of 'this moment of anguish', then burst into tears, and recovered his composure only after a fifteen minute break in the proceedings. After stating that the Tunku had warned him that there would be communal rioting and bloodshed if Singapore did not get out, he announced that 'from today this island shall be for ever a sovereign, democratic and independent nation, founded upon the principles of liberty and justice'.

It seemed that what Sukarno's policy of Confrontation had been unable to achieve in two years of tension and bloodshed had now been achieved through the mistrust and stubbornness of two politicians, each convinced of the justice of his own cause.

In Sarawak and Sabah reaction to the news was immediate. The people were clearly resentful that they had not been consulted before the break was announced. Opposition leaders declared that Malaysia without Singapore was not the Malaysia they had agreed to form. Rumour spread that a Federation of Borneo States, including Brunei, was being canvassed. Only the Tunku's quick reaction and personal visit to the area helped to hold the Borneo states together with Malaysia.

Singapore became a sovereign, independent State within the British Commonwealth and sought entry into the United Nations, sponsored by Malaysia. A few months later, on 2 December, Singapore became a Republic. The question of re-opening trade with Indonesia was tendered but it was made conditional upon Indonesia's recognition of the new state as an independent unit. Sukarno was not ready to accord such recognition in view of the fact that Singapore contained foreign military bases. And the re-opening of trade or diplomatic relations with Indonesia was strongly opposed by Malaysia. It seemed, however, that the Malaysian and Singapore Governments intended to co-operate, as the 2nd Singapore Regiment was flown to Sabah on 18 August to join the Security Forces.

The next move came from the Malaysian Minister of Defence. He announced that Malaysia and Singapore were to seek a new tripartite defence treaty with Britain. It was thought that Australia and New Zealand would continue their associations, as in the past, by making their arrangements through Britain for the use of the Commonwealth Strategic Reserve. Dr Goh Keng Swee, Singapore's new Minister of Defence, was appointed to the Malaysian Central Defence Council. On 2 September the Council decided that Britain should keep the bases, and the Tunku said that new agreements would be negotiated towards the end of the year. Until then it would be madness to move them as they were the only defence against Indonesian aggression. He also stressed that there was no question of Britain using the bases for SEATO purposes.

Mr Denis Healey, Britain's Defence Minister, said during his visit to the area in February 1966 that he expected no difficulties in putting the mutual defence arrangements between Singapore and the United Kingdom on a proper footing.

184

The dust from Singapore's breakaway had hardly settled when news came of a Communist coup in Indonesia. Broadcasting over Djakarta Radio, Lt-Col Untang, a Palace Guard battalion commander, announced that a Revolutionary Council had taken over all powers in Indonesia and had placed Sukarno under 'protective guard'. Their action, he claimed, was to prevent a military coup planned for 5 October by a Generals' Council.

The Revolutionary Council consisted of several pro-Communist officials, including Dr Subandrio, General Omar Dani, Air Force Chief-of-Staff, and Rear-Admiral Martadinata, Navy Chief-of-Staff. Conspicuous by their absence were General Nasution, Commander of the Armed Forces, and Major-General Achmad Yani, the Army Commander. Nasution had long been considered the chief obstacle to a Communist take-over, as the Army had held the balance against the three million strong pro-Peking Communist Party.

The coup took place in the small hours of 1 October 1965. Six generals were kidnapped, including Yani but not Nasution. Sukarno, according to his version, was taken under escort at six in the morning to Halim Air Base which was the Headquarters of the *coup d'état*. His arrival at the Base at 0930 coincided precisely with the moment that his friend and Air Force Commander, Omar Dani, issued an order of the day giving news of the coup. At the same time, elements of the Palace Guard and members of the Communist Youth and Women's organizations (armed and trained by the Air Force) arrived in trucks.

The six kidnapped generals were also brought to the Base and eventually murdered. According to an eye-witness, at least one suffered the vilest tortures and indignities before being killed.

Within five hours of Untang's broadcast, Nasution came on the air to announce that he had crushed the revolt and that the President was safe. Later Sukarno, either voluntarily or under duress, broadcast a message to the country pointing out that the situation was grave and that prompt action was necessary. With the failure of the coup, the President moved to his palace in the hill station of Bogor, some forty miles south of Djakarta. His friend Dani had offered to take him to another sanctuary, but Sukarno refused. This established his 'neutrality'.

During the next ten days events were confused. There was fighting in the streets and many people were killed. The revolt spread to Central Java where the commander, Colonel Suhirman, declared himself for Untang. Fighting later spread to Celebes where the Army reported that it had beaten off an attack by five hundred Communists. Thus failing with an organized coup, the Communists resorted to terrorism, directed particularly against the Muslims. In three weeks one hundred and seventy people were massacred in Central and East Java. Kidnapping, arson, and armed robbery were rampant. In retaliation, anti-Communist moves were instigated throughout the Republic. In the capital, the Communist Party HQ was burned to the ground. The discovery of arms and a transmitter in the building led to mass arrests in the city. Eighteen universities were suspended because of alleged student sympathy for the rebels.

It gradually became clear that, despite frenzied threats to exterminate the powerful PKI, the Army were acting with considerable restraint. In certain localities the Communist organizations were merely suspended.

The PKI, with three million members and perhaps eleven million sympathizers, was still a force to be reckoned with no matter how severely the leaders of the party were purged. Sukarno had always shown leniency towards the PKI in his balancing act between them and the Army. The generals appeared to be saying that Communism in itself was no crime unless it led to treason. Subservience to China was treason. China was accused of complicity in the plot, and the violence of the mobs was directed against Chinese institutions. In Medan, Northern Sumatra, ten thousand chanting Indonesians demonstrated outside the Communist Chinese Consulate, ran down the Chinese flag, and ripped the Consulate emblem from the wall of the building. There was also a threat that Indonesia might break off economic and diplomatic links with China. The number of Indonesian Communists arrested by this time totalled five thousand.

Sukarno returned to Merdeka Palace in Djakarta. His powers had been curtailed by Nasution and General Suharto, but he was still regarded as an essential figurehead. Subandrio, on the other hand, was on the downard path because evidence linked him directly with the Communist coup. Sukarno, however, resisted

186

a growing demand to remove Subandrio altogether. The only step he took was to deprive him of one office, Deputy Chairman of KOTI, giving the job to Nasution. On 16 February 1966 Nasution made an appeal over Djakarta Radio in which he said that the rule of law must prevail in Indonesia. He stated that the PKI had committed terrorism and crimes against the state and must be punished in accordance with the law, otherwise the outside world would regard Indonesia as a country ruled by a dictator. His words followed a strong defence of the PKI made earlier that week by Sukarno who had said that no other party had sacrificed more in the struggle of the Indonesian people for independence.

Within two days of his broadcast, Nasution was out of office. Sukarno, by this time confident that he had ridden the post-coup storm and was once more in a position to take over the complete reins of government, sacked the anti-Communist general. The Army had failed; Nasution had gone; Subandrio was back.

Sukarno was in favour of an early rehabilitation of the out-lawed Communists—now deprived of their long-time leader Aidit who had been killed during the coup. He replaced KOTI (the equivalent of a War Council) with a new organization known as KOGAM (Crush Malaysia Command). Subandrio returned as First Deputy Prime Minister, once more the most senior man after the President.

The establishment of KOGAM indicated that Sukarno and Subandrio, backed by the Communists, were going to intensify their acts of aggression against Malaysia. This was a clever stratagem to divert the attention of the Indonesian people from their domestic and economic troubles. What the Communist coup had failed to do, Sukarno had achieved through political action, removing Nasution and those who stood in the way of the PKI-backed plan to identify the Indonesian Revolution with the Chinese Revolution, making common cause with Communist China through the Peking–Djakarta Axis. Sukarno was once again in a position to join hands with Mao Tse-tung, to defy the world, sneer at the United Nations, and proceed with the establishment of the rival organization CONEFO— Conference of the New Emerging Forces—for which Communist North Korea and Communist North Vietnam had assured their support.

187

Then, early in March, growing resentment throughout the country at the President's attempts to justify the Communist view-point, coupled with exasperation at the rampant inflation, led to student riots in Djakarta. They defied all bans and roamed the city shouting 'Hang Subandrio!' It was perhaps not too late for Sukarno to have exercised his old magic over the mob, but he made one of his most serious blunders. He allowed his Palace Guards to open fire on the students and several were killed. In retaliation the students besieged the Palace, and broke into the Foreign Ministry in undisguised anti-Sukarno rioting.

On 12 March the Army took over again. Sukarno handed over power to General Suharto, retaining only his title. He became a virtual prisoner in his own palace. The new leader's first action was to issue a decree banning the pro-Peking Communist Party. Suharto further pledged that the country would not swing to the extreme Left or the extreme Right. A massive Army demonstration of strength, with tanks, armoured cars, and lorries crammed with troops was welcomed by huge cheering crowds and girls throwing flowers. A full-scale purge of the PKI was launched. The resultant killings have not been accurately assessed, but estimates have reached as high as half a million. There is little doubt that this reign of terror against the Communists and their familes was brought about by the killing of the six generals the previous October, and the dire fear of what the Communists might do in the future. Reliable and responsible Indonesians have expressed the view that had the October coup succeeded the dead on the anti-Communist side would have been numbered in millions.

Power in Indonesia came to rest in three pairs of hands: the Sultan of Jogjakarta, Deputy Premier for Economics, Dr Adam Malik, Foreign Minister, and General Suharto. Nasution returned to the Government as Deputy Supreme Commander of KOGAM. They at once took steps to curb Sukarno's powers. He was no longer allowed direct contact with his ministers without permission of one of the three leaders, and his speeches and press interviews were carefully vetted.

A move was made by the new men for the re-election of Indonesia to the United Nations. Western economic aid was accepted—Britain being among the first to offer a contribution. The 'Crush Malaysia' campaign, however, remained an enigma.

During his early days in office, Suharto had said that it would continue. A few months later Malik dropped hints of a possible end to Confrontation. The query remained: was this a genuine step towards a peaceful situation or a carbon copy of Sukarno's own tactics?

TWENTY-THREE

The Final Stage

The new régime was far from secure. Suharto and his joint deputy prime ministers were faced with a serious problem. On the one hand their need for Confrontation was as great as Sukarno's, since it provided an ideal rallying cry to unite the people behind the new government. On the other hand, the economy was at a very low ebb. More Communists had survived the 'blood bath' than had been liquidated or thrown into prison. In conditions of extreme economic bankruptcy they could still rise again if their organization grew as it had after the 1948 purge. Foreign Minister Malik, it seemed, was keen to bring Confrontation to an end. Not only would this form a basis for economic stability, but might encourage other countries to help refill the coffers of a new 'peace-loving' Indonesia. There could be no harm in at least taking the first steps. On 25 May 1966 eight Indonesian army officers flew to Kuala Lumpur on a goodwill mission, carrying a message from General Suharto stating that Indonesia wished to end Confrontation and make peace with Malaysia. At the airport the Military Mission was met by the Parliamentary Secretary of the Malaysian Ministry of External Affairs. The first Indonesian officer off the plane rushed down the gangway and embraced the Secretary. Both were moved to tears by the occasion.

The mission then flew to Alor Star in north Malaya for talks with the Tunku. Two days later, the Malaysian Deputy Prime Minister had an informal meeting with the Indonesian Foreign Minister at the home of the Thai Foreign Minister in Bangkok. Then their staff got down to the task of finding a formula for peace negotiations. By the end of the month both Ministers were able to exchange sealed packages containing their respective proposals for the end of Confrontation. On 1 June a vague Press statement was issued which gave little away, toasts were drunk in champagne, and Malik led the delegations in Muslim prayer. They then departed to their respective countries and reported to their Governments.

Indonesia had already played the dove on three occasions since the start of Confrontation; nobody could be sure that the fourth 'peace' talks would achieve any more.

For the new régime in Djakarta, the first barrier to be removed was Sukarno. He made a last-ditch speech in defence of his leadership, but instead of the ringing applause which used to greet his words, now the reaction was tepid. On 5 July he was stripped of his title of President For Life, and was to remain President in name only until the next general election. At the same time Communism was outlawed. Sukarno had been prepared to fight for his position, but a tactical move of strong military forces into the regions which may have still favoured him, settled the issue.

With Sukarno defused, Suharto and Malik were ready to confirm the end of Confrontation. In Borneo, steps had already been taken by both sides to cool down the situation across the border and give the peace talks every chance to succeed. Said one British officer, 'The enemy as such was barely existent, and at the same time ever-increasing operational restrictions were placed on the Security Forces as 'Konfrontasi' came to its close— a very frustrating period for all concerned. But at least it gave us the chance to admire and appreciate the scenery for a change.'

All the signs seemed to indicate that this time Indonesia really wished to bring the undeclared war to an end. Early in August, 1966, the Malaysian Deputy Prime Minister, Tun Abdul Razak, and five Cabinet Ministers, flew to Djakarta, where they were met by General Suharto, Malik, and other ministers.

The Peace Agreement was signed by Foreign Minister Adam Malik for Indonesia, and by Tun Abdul Razak for Malaysia. Confrontation ended at noon on 11 August 1966.

The agreement provided for the immediate restoration of diplomatic relations and the exchange of representatives as soon as possible. The Text had four Articles:

1. Malaysia would give the people of Sabah and Sarawak in Borneo an opportunity to re-affirm as soon as practicable at General Elections their previous decision about their status in Malaysia.
2. Immediate diplomatic recognition.

191

3. The cessation of all hostile acts.
4. Stipulation that the Peace Agreement should apply from 11 August.

In Borneo, the so-called 'rebel' factions of the Indonesian forces seemed reluctant to acknowledge the peace agreement, and several groups made attempts to infiltrate into Brunei, Sabah, and Sarawak before ratification in order to establish branches for future internal subversion. A group of fifty entered the Fifth Division heading for Brunei and were told of the signing of the agreement, but continued their march. As a result of operations, forty-one of them were captured. Some escaped but were believed to have died of starvation. By October most of the small groups of incursionists had been demolished.

With the end of Confrontation, British forces started a gradual withdrawal from East Malaysia, handing over control to Malaysian forces. This had already been agreed in August, when Mr Healey, the British Defence Secretary, had told the House of Commons that 10,000 British troops would be withdrawn from Borneo soon after ratification of the Bangkok agreement. In Brunei, however, British forces would still remain, at the Sultan's request.

The campaign in Borneo was a small war by most standards —by those of Korea and Vietnam, a very small war. At peak strength there were only about 17,000 Commonwealth servicemen in Borneo, with another 10,000 immediately available. The service casualties for the whole period were 114 killed and 181 wounded. The civilians suffered 36 killed, 53 wounded, and 4 captured. The Indonesian forces lost at least 590 killed, 222 wounded, and 771 captured.

But Borneo could easily have become another Vietnam. It is in this light that the success of the campaign must be measured. Only leadership of a high quality, and troops of a high standard of training and versatility prevented the conflict from escalating into a full-scale war. From the outset, Walker's aim was to prevent such an escalation. Although the war did go full circle, from mere encounters with small parties of terrorists to conventional warfare at battalion level, it never reached the degree of total war. A major conflict was always possible owing to the added threat of subversion behind the lines with the presence of the 24,000 strong CCO element in the urban areas. This internal threat was kept in check mainly because all commanders had clear orders that if the civil administration and police asked for help they could be given it without prior clearance from the Director of Operations, an important decision because of the need for swift action in putting down internal trouble.

In 1963 and 1964, the Security Forces were fighting terrorists; by the time Walker handed over to General Lea in 1965, they were involved in actions against sophisticated, well-equipped, highly trained, regular soldiers not only dug-in but supported by artillery and mortars. Walker had defeated Sukarno's attempt to tear Borneo apart with guerrilla warfare and internal sabotage and terrorism. The Indonesians were forced into a last-ditch attempt to bring in their regulars, and build up the ferocity of their attacks to the level, at times, of the Burma Campaign. At this final stage, the new Director of Operations was in a more conventional role, and made it clear to his troops that only the highest standards of patrolling, battle-craft, fire and movement, and the fullest use of artillery and mortars could win the day.

The Indonesian regular soldier, although no jungle superman, was a thoroughly competent opponent. He had earned his freedom the hard way against the Dutch (who had been supported by both the British and the Australians). Some of his officers had been trained by the British at the jungle warfare school in Malaya, and the school of intelligence in England. The Indonesian soldier also possessed a variety of modern weapons, and those from behind the iron curtain and the United States were of high quality. He used such weapons as artillery, medium mortars, anti-personnel mines, and rocket-launchers with considerable skill. On the ground, where it finally became a company commander's war, he was beaten by the best of the British, Gurkha and Commonwealth troops, aided by highly efficient command at the top—first Walker and then Lea. In general terms, he was beaten because the Security Forces had the advantage of a major military base in the right place—Singapore, had complete command of the sea and air, and had a superb intelligence service. In the final event he was defeated because the long-drawn-out war ruined the stability and economy of his own country.

INDEX

Service formations are listed in alphabetical order under the heading of 'Security Forces'.

199

SARAWAK *(East Malaysia)* and BRUNEI